HONORING OUR NEIGHBOR'S FAITH

A LUTHERAN PERSPECTIVE ON FAITH TRADITIONS IN AMERICA

REVISED EDITION

AUGSBURG FORTRESS

HONORING OUR NEIGHBOR'S FAITH: A Lutheran Perspective on Faith Traditions in America, Revised Edition

General Editors: Robert Buckley Farlee, Beth Ann Gaede

Cover design: Laurie Ingram
Interior design: Tory Herman
Interior art: Markell Studios

Chapters in this revised edition are based on chapters written for *Honoring Our Neighbor's Faith*, copyright © 1999 by Juleen H. Turnage, Florence Amamoto, Anthony M. Coniaris, Swami Atmavidyananda, Suraiya Mosley Hassan, Rabbi Joseph Edelheit, David A. Lumpp, Robert E. Koenig, and Clyde J. Steckel, and on original material from *Our Neighbor's Faith*, copyright © 1985 Augsburg Publishing House.

Scripture quotations are from New Revised Standard Version Bible, copyright © 1989 Division of Christian Education of the National Council of the Churches of Christ in the United States of America. Used by permission.

ISBN 978-1-5064-0058-7

Manufactured in U.S.A.

CONTENTS

INTRODUCTION

This resource invites us to honor our neighbor's faith. First, it acknowledges that people—especially in pluralistic America—have different beliefs and affirms that those beliefs are worthy of respect. Second, it recognizes that we have difficulty respecting what we do not understand. Indeed, we have seen all too often that disrespect, distrust, and fear of other religious traditions often stem from simple misunderstanding. This is an age-old problem, and Christians have been both perpetrators and victims of such misunderstanding. Early Christians were accused of cannibalism because of confusion regarding the Lord's supper. Present-day Muslims are all too commonly thought to support "holy war" against Christians. Even within Christian communities, perceptions of other denominations are often far from accurate.

In *Honoring Our Neighbor's Faith*, religious groups tell their own story: who they are, what they believe, and how they practice. In many cases, writers from within the traditions agreed to write the essays. In all cases, the chapters were sent to representatives of the groups for their review. We have tried to be fair toward their beliefs, attempting in our editing not to put our slant on their faith. The exception is in the discussion questions, where we encourage Lutherans and others who use this resource to examine the various beliefs in light of their own faith.

How do we deal with differences in beliefs? We honor our neighbor's faith and trust that it is as heartfelt as our own, but where do we go from there? If we are Lutheran, presumably we believe that the Lutheran understanding of God is the most faithful. How, then, do we approach the beliefs of other faith groups? Are they equally faithful, just different? Are they misguided but essentially okay? Are they flat-out wrong? Do we agree with those who say all religious traditions are equally valid understandings of the universal God, or do we agree with those who would insist that Christianity—or, more narrowly, our understanding of Christianity—is the only way to approach God?

These are difficult questions, and people answer them in many ways. Some Christians will not pray even with others whom they acknowledge to be Christian. Other Christians are willing to accept as valid the beliefs of those who have never claimed to be Christian. Still other Christians struggle to deal with groups that follow some Christian practices while also departing from some basic Christian teachings. But as tricky and sometimes wrenching as these questions are, we can be certain that satisfactory answers cannot be found by ignoring or misrepresenting what other faith traditions believe. We need to obtain accurate information and to examine that information respectfully. We must compare what we learn with our own beliefs, and that means we must have a solid understanding of what our own faith asks of us. This resource will help you clarify your own faith tradition and begin to make thoughtful comparisons with others'.

Faith Traditions Explored in This Resource

Hundreds of Christian denominations and dozens of non-Christian traditions have followers in the United States. We tried to choose groups that would represent a wide spectrum of beliefs and that readers are likely to come across because of the group's size or prominent public profile. Of course, you are encouraged to investigate other faiths.

Each essay is accompanied by a table that compares that faith tradition's and the ELCA's core teachings, type of worship, and governance. Following the table are statistics for the number of members and congregations. Readers should keep in mind that the statistics do not offer apples-to-apples comparisons between faith communities, because traditions and even individual congregations do not count members the same way. ELCA congregations, for example, count all who have been received as members of the congregation through baptism or affirmation of baptism. But some congregations carefully distinguish between "active" and "inactive" members (those who do and do not worship or make a donation of record), while others are less rigorous about who is kept on membership rolls. In traditions such as the Assemblies of God, many people hesitate to become a member of a congregation until they no longer have any doubts about their relationship with God, and a person might worship regularly with a congregation for years without ever becoming a member. Other traditions, such as Jewish synagogues and Hindu temples, identify as members those who have paid annual (or, in some communities, lifetime) dues.

Unless otherwise noted, statistics used in this resource are from the *U.S. Religion Census 1952 to 2010*, sponsored by the Association of Statisticians of American Religious Bodies (www.rcms2010.org/compare.php). Other websites offer additional resources for faith community leaders and information about the location, characteristics, and activities of congregations. See especially the following sites for updated information:

Faith Communities Today	www.faithcommunitiestoday.org
Hartford Institute for Religion Research	www.hirr.hartsem.edu
National Congregations Study (NCS)	www.soc.duke.edu/natcong/
Pew Research Center, Religion and Public Life	www.pewforum.org
US Congregational Life Survey (USCLS)	www.uscongregations.org/

Many Christian denominations in the United States belong to one or more of the following organizations, which support a variety of cooperative efforts:

National Association of Evangelicals	www.nae.net
National Council of Churches	www.nationalcouncilofchurches.us
World Council of Churches	www.oikoumene.org

The faith traditions discussed in this resource may be placed in four broad categories, but in some cases you will have to decide which category a given group belongs in. The first category is world religions unrelated to Christianity. This category is clear and comprises the ancient religions of Hinduism (or Vedanta) and Buddhism. The second category is non-Christian world religions with a "family" connection to Christianity. Again, no confusion here: Judaism is the source from which Christianity developed, and Islam is a later religion from the same roots. People will make different calls about which groups belong in the last two categories: Christian denominations and non-Christian denominations with Christian roots. Few observers would question that Episcopalians or Methodists are Christian. Other denominations, though, claim to be Christian, but some of their beliefs raise questions about that identification for some people. Read the essays, look at the tables of comparison, and try to make your own call.

How to Use This Resource

Honoring Our Neighbor's Faith has been designed primarily for adult study groups in Evangelical Lutheran Church in America congregations. Groups are encouraged to use this resource as best fits their circumstances. A group might read through each chapter (perhaps combining some of the shorter ones) and discuss it, beginning with the questions provided. Class members might wish to expand on these presentations by conducting their own research into the history, beliefs, and practices of various groups. Suggestions for further reading, along with website URLs, are provided in each chapter.

You will learn more about both other traditions and your own faith journey if you approach this book and supplementary materials with the goal of furthering your understanding rather than pinpointing beliefs you disagree with or identifying others' "errors." Questions such as the following can be used to guide your exploration and structure your conversation (or reflection if you are reading this book on your own).

The Facts

1. What beliefs or assumptions form the foundation of the denomination or tradition? Think especially about the following:
   - understanding of God
   - understanding of humanity and the human condition
   - origins and nature of a universal problem
   - solution offered for that problem
   - humanity's role in achieving that solution
   - how that solution affects human experience
   - teachings about an afterlife
   - implications of these ideas for daily life

2. What texts, stories, images, symbols, and practices are important in this tradition?

3. What vocabulary do I need to understand?

My Response

1. What surprises or intrigues me?

2. What ideas or practices seem difficult to me?

3. What questions do I have?

Implications

1. What values, beliefs, or practices from this tradition do I admire and wish more people would follow?

2. What elements could Lutherans not incorporate into their own faith and practice, and why?

3. What elements of this tradition are the same as or similar to those of Lutherans? Which ones could ELCA Lutherans comfortably adopt, and why?

4. How have my thoughts and feelings about my own relationship with God and religious values, beliefs, and practices changed as a result of my reflecting on another's?

Where possible, study groups could invite individuals from other traditions to come and speak to the class. Making a trip to worship with (or, if appropriate, simply to observe) the group under discussion could be the best way to get a feel for who they are. If you plan such a visit, contact the group ahead of time, find out if there are any restrictions on dress or behavior, and ask for any hints to help you get more out of your visit. A member of the faith community might serve as a host for your group. Consider inviting a class from that tradition to visit your church, establishing an opportunity for mutual exploration. A noteworthy resource for such visits is *How to Be a Perfect Stranger: The Essential Religious Etiquette Handbook*, 5th ed., Stuart M. Matlins and Arthur J. Magida, (SkyLight Paths, 2011).

We don't expect that all people will agree about who God is and how we should practice our beliefs, even among Christian denominations. We hope, though, that this resource provides accurate information about what others believe and why, that we can gain some insight from other faiths to help us in our own faith journeys, and that without dishonoring our own faith in any way, we can honor our neighbor's faith.

CHAPTER 1

AFRICAN AMERICAN METHODIST CHURCHES

Richard Allen (1760–1831), the founder and first bishop of the African Methodist Episcopal Church, grew up as a slave in Philadelphia.

You probably will not come across a congregation claiming to belong to the "African American Methodist" church body. Rather, this is an umbrella term for a number of denominations that have become important, particularly in the African American community. They include the African Methodist Episcopal Church (AME), the African American Episcopal Zion Church, the Christian Methodist Episcopal Church, and the African Union First Colored Methodist Protestant Church.

These churches have their roots in the Methodist Church, which developed under the leadership of John Wesley, an eighteenth-century Englishman who led what was at first a reforming movement within the Anglican Church. His followers, initially called "Methodists" to mock them, came to accept the name and spread their teachings throughout the world.

Those teachings emphasized sanctification, the process by which the Holy Spirit both leads people to faith and continues to develop their relationship to God. Wesley also promoted the belief that humans have free will to make choices, under the influence of God's grace.

Problems with Discrimination

The Methodist Church became a separate church body in the United States in 1784. While it attracted a wide variety of people, black Christians in particular were drawn to it in part because of John Wesley's strong antislavery statements. He denounced the slave trade, arguing that it was against the will of God. These beliefs at first carried over into the Methodist Church, where members were encouraged to set free any slaves they owned. Unfortunately, as the number of Methodists increased, the church tended to become less outspoken in opposing slavery, especially in the South, where slavery was seen as an indispensable part of life. Of course, slavery wasn't a problem only for Methodists, nor did discrimination occur only in the American South. African Americans in the North experienced it as well.

In reaction to this, African Americans began pulling out of the mother church to form Methodist congregations, and later denominations, where they would be able to participate fully. The first congregation to withdraw for this reason was St. George's Methodist Episcopal Church in Philadelphia in 1787. These actions eventually led to the founding of the African Methodist Episcopal Church in 1816. The African Methodist Episcopal Zion Church was born in 1796, the result of African Americans being denied full participation in a church in New York City. The third of the large African American Methodist bodies was a product of the Reconstruction Era following the American Civil War. In 1870 African American members of the Methodist Episcopal Church, South, asked to form their own church within the larger denomination. Instead, the parent body voted to constitute them as a completely independent denomination that was called the Christian Methodist Episcopal Church.

Believing and Practicing

Reflecting their history, African American Methodist churches maintain doctrines similar to other Methodist bodies. They are trinitarian, looking to God as the creator, Jesus Christ as the Son of God and redeemer of humanity, and the Holy Spirit as the sanctifier. They teach the sinfulness of humans and their need for repentance, as well as reliance on God's grace for salvation. At the same time, the churches teach that faith in God should lead to lives that reflect the indwelling of the Holy Spirit.

Worship in the African American Methodist churches blends Methodist forms with African American styles. The music is generally spirited, including gospel, spirituals, and European-based hymns. A choir usually leads the singing and may be accompanied by piano, organ, drums, and other instruments.

The term *episcopal* in the name of most of these denominations means that they are headed by a bishop. This is also the case among other Methodist denominations and reflects their Anglican heritage, as well as biblical roots. Congregations, however, have a great deal of autonomy in choosing their own forms of ministry.

Members of these churches put their beliefs into practice in their communities. The congregation is often a center of neighborhood life, and its ministries extend far beyond worship to meet the everyday needs of the people around them. The church building may be a place to feed the hungry, care for children, discuss community concerns, and collect clothing for local or foreign needs. The African American Methodist churches have helped to meet an important need, both historically and in the present day.

For Discussion

1. In what ways is having churches made up primarily of one ethnic heritage (whether it is white, African American, Asian, Hispanic, or another) helpful? In what ways could it be harmful?

2. Clearly the church sinned when it discriminated against African Americans. What such problems do we see in churches now?

3. Churches such as the African American Methodist denominations challenge others to become involved in their communities. How is your congregation meeting that challenge?

For Further Study

· *African Methodist Episcopal Zion Church, 1972–1996: A Bicentennial Commemorative History* by James Clinton Hoggard (AME Zion Publishing House, 1998)

· *Fortress Introduction to Black Church History* by Anne H. Pinn and Anthony B. Pinn (Augsburg, 2001)

· *Songs of Zion: The African Methodist Episcopal Church in the U.S. and South Africa* by James T. Campbell (University of North Carolina Press, 1998)

·

· Websites
  - African Methodist Episcopal Church: www.ame-church.com
  - African Methodist Episcopal Zion Church: www.amez.org
  - Christian Methodist Episcopal Church: thecmechurch.org

Table of Comparison

	African American Methodists	Lutherans
Teachings	1. Believe the Bible contains the word of God. 2. Teach justification by faith. 3. Consider baptism and holy communion not only symbolically, but also as signs of God's grace. 4. Believe the church should express its faith in concrete action in the affairs of the world.	1. Accept the Bible as the written witness to God's revelation of saving action through Jesus Christ. 2. Same. 3. Consider baptism and holy communion as means of conveying God's grace. 4. Believe the church lives to preach the gospel and celebrate the sacraments, giving strength for service in the world.
Type of Worship	Quite free and emotional, though often based on liturgical patterns.	Liturgical, following the primary pattern of the Western church.
Governance	Episcopal, with bishop but no claim to apostolic succession. Congregations quite free within clearly defined parameters.	Interdependent congregational, regional, national, and global expressions of the church are characterized by democratic decision making, strong ecumenical relationships, elected leadership, and an ordained ministry.
Statistics*	Membership: 1,601,288 Congregations: 7,375	

*Figures for the three largest bodies in the United States

CHAPTER 2

ASSEMBLIES OF GOD

Worship featuring prayer and praise is characteristic of Assemblies of God congregations.

The Assemblies of God is one of several Pentecostal denominations in the United States. As one of the largest of these groups, the Assemblies of God has more than thirty million believers in all parts of the world.

The term *Pentecostal* comes from the experience of Jesus' disciples on Pentecost when the Holy Spirit came on them (Acts 2). This event has been interpreted in various ways, but Pentecostals understand it as a baptism in the Holy Spirit that brought its recipients certain special gifts. Christians continued to experience this outpouring of the Holy Spirit from time to time throughout history, and it reemerged in the early days of the twentieth century when a Pentecostal revival swept the world and touched all denominations. Many believers began receiving this baptism in the Holy Spirit, including the initial evidence of "speaking in tongues." At first there was no organization; however, in 1914 the Assemblies of God was formed, and various other Pentecostal groups also began.

Theologically, the Assemblies of God is Arminian, stressing the free will of human beings. The church teaches that humankind fell into sin and needs salvation. The believer's part is to repent and believe Christ died for one's sins; then God forgives. In the new birth, at salvation, Jesus Christ comes to dwell by his Spirit within the new believer.

Worship in Assemblies of God churches tends to be informal, with the service focusing on preaching the word of God. The Bible is affirmed as verbally inspired of God and the authority for faith and conduct in the Christian's life. Two ordinances are practiced: water baptism by immersion as a confession of faith after a person has accepted Christ as Savior, and the Lord's supper or communion.

The Assemblies of God does not belong to the World Council or National Council of Churches; however, it is a member of the National Association of Evangelicals, the Pentecostal/Charismatic Churches of North America, the Pentecostal World Conference, and the World Assemblies of God Fellowship.

The church subscribes to four core beliefs: salvation, divine healing, baptism in the Holy Spirit, and Jesus' second coming. The church sponsors benevolent and social ministries, such as Teen Challenge (a drug rehabilitation program with centers worldwide), programs for children and youth, Compact Family Services, feeding programs conducted through congregations, and

Convoy of Hope (a volunteer mobilization organization that works among people who are poor). However, these are not viewed as the major mission of the denomination. Rather, the Assemblies of God is committed to fulfilling a fourfold mission: (1) evangelize people who are lost, (2) worship God, (3) disciple believers, and (4) show compassion. The church teaches that God, through salvation, is able to change an individual and will thus transform society through changed people.

For Discussion

1. The Assemblies of God has grown rapidly in recent years. What do you think are some reasons for this growth?

2. Pentecostals place a greater emphasis on certain gifts of the Holy Spirit (see 1 Corinthians 12:4ff.) than do some other Christians. How might such an emphasis change your relationship with God?

3. While Lutherans speak of sacraments as means of grace, the Assemblies of God understands baptism and the Lord's supper as ordinances. Find out how the meanings of these terms differ. How are they the same? Would thinking of baptism and the Lord's supper as ordinances change their meaning for you?

For Further Study

· *The Assemblies of God: Godly Love and the Revitalization of American Pentecostalism* by Margaret M. Poloma and John C. Green (New York University Press, 2010)

· Available through the Assemblies of God website
  - "Statement of Fundamental Truths," the sixteen tenets of faith taught by the denomination
  - Small group curriculum with one session on each of the four core beliefs
  - Suggested books, articles, sermons, and media on the four core beliefs

· Assemblies of God website: ag.org

Table of Comparison

	Assemblies of God	Lutherans
Teachings	1. Believe the Bible is the completely inspired word of God.	1. Believe the Bible is the written witness to God's revelation of saving action through Jesus Christ.
	2. Practice two ordinances: baptism by immersion and the Lord's supper.	2. Celebrate two sacraments: baptism and the Lord's supper.
	3. Believe in an experience following salvation called "baptism in the Holy Spirit" with speaking in tongues.	3. Believe the Holy Spirit is given in baptism. Speaking in tongues is the least of the gifts of the Spirit.
	4. Accept the triune nature of God and the divinity of Christ.	4. Same.
	5. Believe Christ's death provided healing for the body as well as salvation for the soul.	5. View bodily healing as usually occurring through normal medical care.

Type of Worship	Free and informal with hymns, prayers, and preaching. Spontaneous testimonies are sometimes included.	Orderly liturgical patterns with varying roles for pastors, other lay leaders, and the congregation.
Governance	Fellowship of independent congregations are organized into districts, usually following state lines.	Interdependent congregational, regional, national, and global expressions of the church are characterized by democratic decision making, strong ecumenical relationships, elected leadership, and an ordained ministry.
Statistics	Membership: 2,944,887 Congregations: 12,258	

CHAPTER 3

BAPTIST CHURCHES

Baptists are known for baptizing adult believers by immersion.

The name Baptist denotes one of the chief characteristics of Baptists—their doctrine of baptism. Baptists accept believer's baptism but reject infant baptism. People who came to be known as Baptists were led to this doctrine of baptism by their study of the New Testament, where they found instances of believer's baptism but failed to find any instances of infant baptism.

Baptist Beginnings

Baptist historians are not in agreement about Baptist beginnings. Some early historians believed that Baptists began with John the Baptist and repeatedly reemerged as various sects within the church. Other historians regard these groups as forerunners of Baptists and believe that Baptists really began among Separatists from the Church of England who were influenced by Dutch Mennonites in the early seventeenth century.

What seems beyond doubt is that during the Reformation of the sixteenth century, two contrasting views emerged regarding what changes the church needed to undergo. One was reformation: the view of Martin Luther, Ulrich Zwingli, John Calvin, and the reformers of the church in England. The other was restitution: the restoration of the first-century church as depicted in the New Testament. This was the view of the Anabaptists, such as Conrad Grebel, George Blaurock, Balthazar Hübmaier, and Felix Manz.

Although the first Anabaptists—so named by their opponents, who regarded them as re-(*ana*) baptizers—were baptized as infants, they also baptized one another as believers. By this action they separated themselves from the other churches of the Reformation era to form so-called pure churches, that is, churches consisting of Christian believers who had undergone believer's baptism. But just as there were various kinds of Lutherans, so there were various kinds of Anabaptists. At the one extreme were the militant Anabaptists of the city of Munster in Germany, who in 1534 tried to restore the "pure church" by violence. At the other extreme were the mild Anabaptists, such as Menno Simons of Holland, who founded the Mennonites.

A group of these Dutch Mennonites, the Waterlander Mennonites, strongly influenced the group that became the first English Baptists. In its early history, the Church of England was torn between factions favorable to the Roman Catholic Church and those who wanted to split from Rome. Queen Elizabeth I resolved to end this tension by establishing a church of the "middle way" between Protestantism and Catholicism. But this middle way did not satisfy everybody, and some Protestants began to separate from the Church of England. These Separatist groups were often persecuted, and in 1608 one such group, led by John Smyth, emigrated to Amsterdam, Holland. There they were influenced by the Waterlander Mennonites to reject infant baptism and practice only believer's baptism. Smyth then baptized himself and other members of his group. He became a Mennonite and died in Holland. Other members of his group declined to become Mennonites, and in 1612, led by Thomas Helwys, they returned to England to form the first Baptist church on English soil at Spitalfields near London.

These earliest English Baptists were Arminian in theology; that is, they believed that God desires to save all people and that salvation depends on both divine grace and human free will. They further believed that each congregation should be independent of both church and state authority. The English Baptists formed voluntary associations of congregations for mutual help and became known as General Baptists. Other Baptists, however, accepted the Calvinistic idea that God predetermines that certain people shall be saved and others lost. These Calvinistic Baptists became known as Particular Baptists.

Baptists in the United States

The earliest Baptists in the United States came from England to New England and from there spread throughout the states. In 1630 Roger Williams, not yet a Baptist but a devotee of religious liberty, fled to Massachusetts to escape persecution in England. However, Williams was similarly forced to flee from there to Native American territory surrounding Massachusetts, where he founded the city of Providence and the state of Rhode Island. He was able to obtain a charter for the new state that guaranteed religious liberty. From Rhode Island, Baptists gradually spread throughout the United States, forming associations as in England.

Like other Protestant denominations, Baptists became divided by the tensions of the Civil War period. Already in 1845 Baptists in the southern states founded the Southern Baptist Convention. Baptists in the northern states, while maintaining local associations, were slower to unite. In 1907, however, they formed the Northern Baptist Convention, which was later renamed the American Baptist Convention, and later still the American Baptist Churches. Since that time, other divisions have led to the formation of additional associations.

A large number of African Americans were attracted to the Baptist churches, but they were not welcome in the white churches or conventions. They formed their own conventions, such as the National Baptist Convention, the National Convention, Inc., and the Progressive Baptist Convention. There has been some progress in integrating the Baptist bodies, and some African American churches have fairly close relations with the American Baptist Churches.

Basic Baptist Principles

Despite their differences and divisions, most Baptists have throughout their history held four principles in common:

- the restitution or restoration of the New Testament church in later times, including our own; the restitution, that is, of a regenerate church membership;
- the practice of believer's baptism only, without infant baptism, as a means of restoring the New Testament church and keeping it pure;
- a congregational structure in which each member has a vote and each congregation is independent of the others, though free to enter into association with others while maintaining its autonomy;

· a commitment to defending religious freedom, including the freedom of the congregation within the denomination, the freedom of each denomination to make its own decisions without pressure from any other denomination, and the freedom of each congregation and each denomination from the state.

In addition to these four principles, two others define Baptist belief, particularly in the Southern Baptist Convention:

· a reliance on the New Testament teaching of the priesthood of all believers, whereby all Christians have direct access to God, not mediated by clergy;

· an insistence that scripture, often interpreted quite literally, provides the sole authority for teaching and belief.

Baptist Theology

Basic Baptist principles are clear, but Baptist theology is extremely varied. This is due in part to the Baptist stress on religious freedom and in part to doing without creeds and confessions of faith.

Unlike most Christian denominations, Baptists in general do not use the ancient Christian creeds either in worship or in Christian education. They see themselves as confessional (in a broad sense) rather than creedal. However, Baptists have from time to time adopted statements of belief.

Like most other Protestant denominations, Baptists understand the authority of the Bible in different ways. Baptist fundamentalists believe that the Bible is the direct word of God and therefore inerrant. Other Baptists, however, believe that the Bible is the word of God mediated through the word of human beings—prophets, psalmists, historians, apostles, and evangelists—and therefore not inerrant.

Baptists retain two ordinances, baptism and the Lord's supper. Baptists insist that only a person who already has faith in Christ may be baptized. Believer's baptism is understood by most Baptists to be a sign, not a means, of salvation. Baptists also practice the supper, generally following the understanding that the supper is a memorial meal only and not a means of grace.

Baptists and Ecumenism

Baptists participate in ecumenism in varying degrees. Some are deeply concerned about peace and justice in the world; others have little interest in these issues. Some are concerned with interreligious dialogue and are willing to learn from other religions; others are not. On the question of Christian unity, some Baptists would reject any dialogue, collaboration, or union with other denominations, regarding them as false churches. Others would allow for dialogue or collaboration (seeing some degree of validity in the other denominations), but still refuse to unite with other groups. And a few Baptist churches favor participating in organizations such as the Consultation on Church Union, as well as reconsidering and possibly modifying traditional Baptist principles.

For Discussion

1. What do infant and believer's baptism say about how God is understood to be at work in the person?

2. How important do you think it is that the present-day church be closely modeled on the first-century church? Why?

3. How do you think the use or nonuse of creeds might influence a denomination's understanding of church unity? What other factors could affect the meaning of unity?

For Further Study

- *Baptists in America: A History* by Thomas S. Kidd and Barry Hankins (Oxford University Press, 2015)
- *Baptist Ways: A History* by Bill J. Leonard (Judson, 2003)
- *In Search of the New Testament Church: The Baptist Story* by C. Douglas Weaver (Mercer University Press, 2008)
- Websites
  - American Baptist Churches USA: www.abc-usa.org
  - National Baptist Convention, USA: www.nationalbaptist.com
  - Southern Baptist Convention: www.sbcnet.org

Table of Comparison

	Baptists	Lutherans
Teachings	1. Accept the Bible as the word of God. Some conservative Baptists are very literal in interpretation. 2. Accept no creeds, with each person to interpret the Bible for himself or herself. Refuse to use creeds as a "test of faith." 3. Practice only believer's baptism. 4. Believe immersion is the only scriptural method of baptism. 5. Practice two ordinances: baptism and the Lord's supper. Communion considered a sign of salvation.	1. Accept the Bible as the written witness to God's revelation of saving action through Jesus Christ. 2. Accept the historic creeds as definitions and summaries of biblical truth. 3. Baptize both infants and adults. 4. Practice baptism by water in the name of the Father, Son, and Holy Spirit, regardless of method (submersion, immersion, or pouring). 5. Practice two sacraments: baptism and holy communion as God's means of conveying God's grace.
Type of Worship	Free and generally unstructured, according to choice of congregation and minister.	Liturgical pattern based on tradition of the Western church.
Governance	Congregational form regarded as the only scriptural type. Some joint work carried out through conventions.	Interdependent congregational, regional, national, and global expressions of the church are characterized by democratic decision making, strong ecumenical relationships, elected leadership, and an ordained ministry.
Statistics*	Membership: 24,846,464 Congregations: 66,873	

*Figures for the ten largest Baptists denominations in the United States

CHAPTER 4

BUDDHISM

Buddhism features many forms of meditation. All forms of meditation seek ultimately to allow the practitioner to let go of his or her ego.

Trying to describe Buddhism is a little like trying to describe a snowflake—or Christianity. Buddhism has taken many forms in its twenty-five-hundred year history. Some forms of Buddhism are nontheistic, while the adherents of other forms pray to various "gods." Some emphasize meditation, while others argue that only faith matters. This proliferation of forms—schools, branches, sects—was the result of Buddhism's inclusiveness and openness, which led to a tendency to absorb local cultures and religious forms as it spread from India to Southeast Asia, China, Korea, Japan, and Tibet. This adaptability has made Buddhism enormously successful; more than 50 percent of the world's population lives in areas where Buddhism has been the dominant religious force at some time. Despite repression in Communist countries, it is still the major religion in most of Asia. All forms of Buddhism have the same root, however: the life and teachings of Gautama (or Gotama) Buddha.

The Historical Buddha

Buddha is a title that means "one who has been awakened" or "the Enlightened One." Although it might be applied to any wise being (Buddhism recognizes both incarnated and nonincarnated, or "celestial," buddhas), it has traditionally been reserved for that rare individual who has a transcendent and transformative insight into the nature of reality. Any person has the potential to become a buddha, though the title has usually been used to refer to the historical Buddha, Gautama Buddha.

Gautama Buddha was born as Siddhartha, a prince of the Sakya clan, in what is now Nepal near its border with India. Although the date is controversial, most scholars think Siddhartha was born around 566 BCE. Siddhartha's father belonged to a warrior caste and was a governor of the area in which he lived, so Siddhartha was raised in comfort. As time passed, he grew up, married, and had a son. At the age of twenty-nine, he left home and family to start a spiritual quest to understand the suffering he saw around him. He studied with religious teachers and learned ascetic practices that he followed strictly for six years. He finally realized, however, that these practices were not leading him closer to enlightenment, so he abandoned them. Alone, meditating under a Bodhi tree, he reached enlightenment at the age of thirty-five. Siddhartha, now *Sakyamuni* (meaning "the sage of the Sakya clan") or Gautama Buddha, went to Benares, India, where he preached his first sermon. He devoted the next forty-five years to wandering and preaching in northern India, spending the rainy season (June to September) in a monastery. He attracted many disciples, both lay and monastic, men and women. He died a peaceful and natural death at eighty years old.

The Heart of the Buddha's Teaching

At the core of all forms of Buddhism are the Four Noble Truths and the Eightfold Path, the heart of Gautama's insights into reality and especially the human condition.

The first Noble Truth is that *life is suffering*. This does not mean that there are no moments of happiness, but that these moments are not permanent. Even the most fortunate of us inevitably experiences disappointment.

The second Noble Truth is that *there is a reason for this suffering*. Suffering obviously may be caused by painful events—not getting the job we wanted or losing a friend, for instance—but these events cause suffering because of our underlying desire and attachment. We suffer because we can't always get what we want. We suffer when we lose a person to whom we were attached. Because of this attachment, in fact, suffering is inevitable because life is change. There is no way indefinitely to prolong life, much less happy moments.

But isn't it human nature to desire and to become attached to things and to people? Of course! Does this mean that suffering is inevitable and that we just need to accept it? Here the Buddha's answer was no. The third Noble Truth is that *there is a way to end suffering*, and the fourth Noble Truth is that *the way to end suffering is the Eightfold Path*.

The Eightfold Path can be arranged under three headings: wisdom, morality, and concentration.

Wisdom
· Right Views—understanding the Buddha's teachings and Truth/Reality.
· Right Aspirations—high and noble aims.

Morality
· Right Speech—speaking kind words and truth; not lying, gossiping, or being verbally abusive.
· Right Conduct—good, moral, compassionate behavior.
· Right Livelihood—having an honest living that does not cause suffering to others.

Concentration
· Right Effort—perseverance in goodness and clearing the mind.
· Right Mindfulness—attentiveness to reality and the present moment.
· Right Meditation—concentration on Buddha and the *Dharma* (Buddha's teachings and the basic truth of things), using meditation as an instrument to attain enlightenment.

Like the Ten Commandments, all elements of the Eightfold Path need to be practiced simultaneously; there is no linear progression. There seems to be a logical order, though, in that the first two steps have to do with coming to understand the Buddha's teachings and wanting to improve one's life, the next three have to do with moral action in everyday life, and the last three have to do with practices that deepen understanding of life and reality. However, one can practice Right Conduct, for instance, without understanding Buddha's teachings or meditating.

Clearly, though, the practices reinforce and deepen each other. Following the Eightfold Path leads to Nirvana, the cessation of suffering. Although Nirvana is sometimes depicted as a place (comparable to heaven) in paintings and literature, it can also be seen as the state of highest consciousness, a perfect understanding of reality. Rejecting the extreme ascetic practices then in use, Buddha taught a "way of moderation," a "middle way," placing enlightenment and salvation from suffering within reach of ordinary people as well as monastic followers.

Other Principal Buddhist Concepts

Buddha-Nature and *Bodhisattvas.* Buddhism teaches that all people have a buddha-nature, a spark of the divine; however, most of us have a hard time getting in touch with and expressing that spark because our ego and desires distort our vision of reality and our ability to respond to others purely and altruistically.

The various practices taught to reach enlightenment are aimed at erasing the ego and attachment in order to help us see reality more clearly and get in touch with that spark of the divine. Reaching enlightenment is like dispelling the clouds covering the sun. As a transcendent understanding of reality, it leads naturally to wisdom and compassion. The ideal person, especially in Mahayana Buddhism, is the *bodhisattva*, one who reaches enlightenment but remains in human form to teach and lead others to Nirvana. Bodhisattva, like Buddha, is a title. Thus, Jesus, for instance, could be considered a bodhisattva.

Karma. Karma is the law of cause and effect: as you sow, so shall you reap. But what about those people who seem to get away with evil deeds? Some forms of Buddhism believe in reincarnation, that deeds done in this life may affect future lives even when the law of karma seems not to have "worked" in the short run. These Buddhists believe one is especially lucky to be born human, because it is in this form that one has the most freedom to create (and improve) one's destiny. But on a psychological level, the law of karma is always operating in that our actions affect who we are; that is, by doing good things, we become better people.

Meditation and Egolessness. Many forms of Buddhism teach various forms of meditation with perhaps seemingly different goals—emptying or focusing the mind or sending loving-kindness, for instance. However, at base, all forms of meditation seek ultimately to allow the practitioner to rise above or let go of his or her ego. Have you ever had an experience where you were so caught up in something that you didn't notice the time passing? This is a glimpse of the experience of egolessness. *No self* does not mean having no personality, but being released from the anxieties and distortions caused by the ego, which limits us, to see reality more clearly and to go with the flow of the moment more purely, to be a better conduit for the boundless love and energy of the universe.

Mindfulness. Meditation is also a practice in *mindfulness*, paying attention to the present moment. Every moment presents the opportunity to see reality more deeply and clearly, but most of the time we are too preoccupied by our own concerns to pay attention to what is *really* around us. Meditation is not emphasized in all Buddhist schools, however, because Buddhists believe that any act—sweeping the floor or washing the dishes—if done mindfully can be a sacred act, a path toward enlightenment. The Buddha avoided the dogmatism of his age, and Buddhism generally teaches that specific religious practices are not important as long as the aims are not lost.

Development of Buddhism

Before his death, the Buddha is reported to have told his followers that thereafter the Dharma (that is, "the Teachings") would be their teacher. These teachings are contained in the *Tripitakas* (translated "the Three Baskets"). The Sutra Pitaka contains the addresses and sermons for the laity. The Vinaya Pitaka contains the rules of conduct for the monks and their communities. The Abhidharma Pitaka was a later development (starting about 350 BCE) containing the metaphysics and philosophy of Buddhism in a more systematic fashion. These teachings were originally handed down orally, with more attention paid to their content than to the actual words. Disciples were allowed to recite the scriptures in their own dialects. Versions of the canon exist in Sanskrit, Pali, Chinese, Japanese, and Tibetan, the Sanskrit and Pali texts reflecting its Indian origins; the others, its transmission to other Asian countries.

Buddhism got a tremendous boost from its enthusiastic adoption in the third century BCE by King Ashoka in India. Ashoka had authority over a great part of southern Asia and sent many missionaries. By the first century CE, Buddhism was a powerful force in India and Sri Lanka (formerly Ceylon). From these roots, Buddhism was introduced by trade routes to Southeast Asia, China (first century), Korea (fourth century), Japan (sixth century), and Tibet (seventh century). Buddhism was so successful because its openness allowed it to assimilate local cultural and religious practices. Also, different sects could emphasize different elements in the teachings; however, most forms of Buddhism can be associated with one of three main branches: Hinayana (Southern), Mahayana (Eastern), and Tantric (Northern) Buddhism.

Hinayana Buddhism emphasizes the attainment of enlightenment through self-power, following the example of Gautama Buddha. This form of Buddhism is the oldest and most conservative form of Buddhism and is most prevalent in India, Sri Lanka, and Southeast Asia (Burma, Cambodia, Laos, and Thailand). Mahayana Buddhism arose in the second century after the death of Buddha, splitting from the Hinayana schools, and emphasizes the need for help from another power and the potential for anyone to become a bodhisattva. This more liberal form of Buddhism is prevalent in China, Korea, Japan, Vietnam, Tibet, and Mongolia. Tantric Buddhism emphasizes more mystical and magical elements, such as the use of mandalas and mantras. Tantric forms of Buddhism coexist with others schools of Buddhism, most notably in Tibet.

Buddhism Comes to America

Although Buddhism spread throughout Asia, it was slow to come to the West. Buddhist (and Hindu) ideas were introduced through transcendentalist writers such as Ralph Waldo Emerson and Henry David Thoreau, as well as theosophists in the nineteenth century, but knowledge of Buddhism was sketchy and imperfect. Buddhism as a religion came to America with the Chinese immigrants who worked on the railroads and in the gold fields of the West in the mid-nineteenth century. Buddhism was further strengthened with the Japanese immigration to Hawaii and the West Coast at the turn of the twentieth century. This immigration led to the founding of ethnic Buddhist temples. The first Buddhist temple in the United States was the First Chinese Buddhist Temple, founded in San Francisco in 1853. The Japanese community started the Buddhist Mission of North America (which became the Buddhist Churches of America) in San Francisco in 1899.

From the late nineteenth century on, Buddhism gradually achieved a wider American audience. Japanese teachers brought Zen Buddhism, a sect of the Mahayana branch, to this country, and it became especially widely known in the 1950s and 1960s. The late 1960s saw the establishment of groups founded by Tibetan Buddhists led by charismatic leaders, and the 1970s saw a revived interest in another sect known as Theravada Buddhism but with a new emphasis on *Vipassana* (loving-kindness) meditation.

Buddhism in America: Zen and Shin Buddhism

When Americans think of Buddhism, the images that generally come to mind are monks in orange robes from Southeast Asia or Tibet or people doing Zen meditation. The former image springs from television programs and knowledge of world affairs, the latter from the tremendous popularity of Zen among Americans.

Zen's popularity in America was helped by its adoption by the Beats in the 1950s and the counterculture in the 1960s. Writers such as Allen Ginsberg, Jack Kerouac, Gary Snyder, and

Robert Pirsig helped increase Zen's visibility. One of the important elements to notice here is that all of these writers are white. White American Buddhists tend to follow one of three traditions—Zen, Tibetan, or Vipassana Buddhism. All of these sects emphasize meditation as the path to enlightenment, with the result that many Americans mistakenly equate Buddhism with meditation. The emphasis that these sects place on self-reliance, "virtuoso" spiritual practices (long meditation retreats, for instance), and enlightenment as a goal appeals to competitive and individualistic America—particularly highly educated, middle- to upper-class white Americans.

By contrast, the other most prevalent form of Buddhism in America is almost invisible: Shin Buddhism, often considered the "protestant" wing of Buddhism because of its insistence that the key to Nirvana is faith, rather than any rigorous ritual or strict ascetic practice. Shin Buddhism is little known because it is almost totally an ethnic religion brought to the United States by Japanese immigrants (mostly farmers who were poor). Discouraged from assimilation in the first half of the twentieth century by prejudice and discrimination, first-generation Japanese Americans nurtured Japanese culture and values in their children through the Buddhist temple. But farsighted early church leaders also encouraged Americanization, blending East and West by adapting hymns, developing Sunday school programs, and organizing Boy Scout troops. The Buddhist Churches of America is now more than one hundred years old and has spread nationwide. However, because Shin Buddhism has remained mainly an ethnic church, the numbers have been decreasing as more and more Japanese Americans marry people who are not Japanese.

Buddhism in America grew steadily in the second half of the twentieth century. There were many reasons for this, including the general increased interest in spirituality in general in our very materialistic and secularized society; however, some of the reasons can be found within Buddhism itself. The goal of enlightenment, the idea of karma, and the Buddha's encouragement to test the teachings of the Buddha against one's experience and not rely on tradition, dogma, or authority parallel America's generally experiential and scientific worldview. The Buddha did not concern himself with questions such as who created the universe, but focused only on what he believed was essential for spiritual development. This focus on the practical also appeals to our more skeptical age. Furthermore, Buddhism's philosophical and psychological understanding and sophistication are attractive to many people.

Despite repression in many Communist countries, Buddhism remains a vital force in the world today, especially in Asia but increasingly in North America. Buddhists observe that after twenty-five hundred years, the Buddha's teachings remain as profound and relevant as ever and that Buddhism has much to offer people of all faiths in understanding the human condition and the causes and cures for suffering.

For Discussion

1. What aspects of Buddhism are attractive to you, and why?

2. Generally speaking, Buddhism is inclusive of other faiths, while Christianity historically has presented itself as the only way to salvation. What factors may have contributed to these different approaches?

3. Though it is an ancient religion, Buddhism was slow to catch on in the West, yet now it is attracting many followers here. Why do you think this is so?

For Further Study

· *Buddha* by Karen Armstrong (Penguin, 2004)

· *Buddhism: A Concise Introduction* by Huston Smith and Phillip Novak (Harper, 2003)

· *Destructive Emotions: A Scientific Dialogue with the Dalai Lama* by Daniel Goleman (Bantam, 2008)

- *An Introduction to Buddhism: Teachings, History and Practices*, 2nd ed., by Peter Harvey (Cambridge University Press, 2013)
- *Living Buddha, Living Christ* by Thich Nhat Hanh and Elaine Pagels (Riverhead, 2007)
- *Zen Mind, Beginner's Mind* by Shunryu Suzuki, ed. Trudy Dixon (Shambhala, 2011)

Table of Comparison

	Buddhists	Lutherans
Teachings	1. Understand "God" as ultimate reality, the All. Not concerned with how the universe was created. 2. See the goal of Buddhism as enlightenment (perfect understanding of reality, which leads to compassion for all beings) and Nirvana (cessation of suffering). 3. Believe in the Four Noble Truths and the Eightfold Path, but are encouraged to test teachings against their own experience. 4. Believe all people have a Buddha-nature, the potential to become a buddha or bodhisattva (like Gautama Buddha or Jesus). 5. Believe in karma, the law of cause and effect. Many Buddhists also believe in reincarnation.	1. Believe in a personal, triune God—Father (creator), Son (redeemer), Holy Spirit (sanctifier). 2. See Christian life as living in God's grace and loving God and others. 3. Believe God's will is revealed in the scriptures in law and gospel; though interpreted in everyday living, these teachings are unchanging. 4. Believe Jesus is the unique Son of God; we are encouraged to imitate his faithfulness. Our salvation was won through his death and resurrection. 5. Teach that although humans have freedom to disobey God and their actions have effects, all is under the umbrella of God's law and grace. Each human has one earthly life.
Type of Worship	Varies according to sect. Most common elements are chanting, an incense offering, silent meditation, and a talk by a priest or monk.	Liturgical pattern based on tradition of the Western church.
Governance	Varies. Some Buddhist sects are directed by teachers; others are less hierarchical.	Interdependent congregational, regional, national, and global expressions of the church are characterized by democratic decision making, strong ecumenical relationships, elected leadership, and an ordained ministry.
Statistics	Membership: 991,683 Congregations: 2,854	

CHAPTER 5

CHRISTIAN AND MISSIONARY ALLIANCE

Hymn singing is an important part of the free and informal worship services in Alliance churches.

The Christian and Missionary Alliance was founded by Albert B. Simpson, a Presbyterian minister who felt called to evangelize the masses of New York City and to send missionaries to preach the gospel in foreign lands.

In 1887 Simpson organized an interdenominational fellowship called the Christian Alliance and an international missionary society called the Evangelical Missionary Alliance. These two were combined in 1897 as the Christian and Missionary Alliance.

The Alliance sponsors more than 750 international missionaries who are serving in sixty-seven countries in Asia, Africa, South America, and the Middle East, as well as special ministries in Europe. This vast missionary program is supported mainly by Alliance churches in the United States and Canada.

The Alliance World Fellowship (AWF), of which the Christian and Missionary Alliance in the United States is a member, has fifteen thousand churches and 2.4 million members and with its partners has a presence in more than eighty nations and territories. The AWF is a consultative organization that sponsors international missions projects and meets quadrennially for mutual exchange of information and encouragement.

The Alliance is evangelical and conservative in its theology. Above all, it is Christ-centered. This is reflected in its teaching of the *fourfold gospel*: Christ our Savior; Christ our Sanctifier; Christ our Healer; and Christ our Coming King.

It affirms that the Old and New Testaments, inerrant as originally given, were verbally inspired by God and are a complete revelation of God's will for the salvation of humankind. The scriptures constitute the divine and only rule of Christian faith and practice.

Alliance churches conduct free and informal worship services that include hymn singing, prayer, and the reading of the scriptures. A prominent place is always given to the preaching of the word. Two ordinances are practiced: baptism and the Lord's supper. Baptism is only for adults and young people as a testimony of their faith.

For Discussion

1. Reflecting its name, the Christian and Missionary Alliance places a large emphasis on foreign missions. What do you know about your own church's mission outreach? How does it compare with the work of the Alliance?

2. Look at the fourfold gospel above. Which of these titles for Christ do you think your church would stress the most?

3. Compare the Alliance's understanding of baptism with that of your church.

For Further Study

· *All for Jesus: God at Work in the Christian and Missionary Alliance for More than 125 Years*, by Robert L. Niklaus, John S. Sawin, and Samuel J. Stoesz (Christian, 2013)

· *Genuine Gold: The Cautiously Charismatic Story of the Early Christian and Missionary Alliance* by Paul L. Kin (Word and Spirit, 2006)

· Christian and Missionary Alliance website: www.cmalliance.org

Table of Comparison

	Christian and Missionary Alliance	Lutherans
Teachings	1. Believe in the inerrancy of the Bible as originally given.	1. Accept the Bible as the written witness to God's revelation of saving action through Jesus Christ.
	2. Affirm the triune nature of God.	2. Same.
	3. Accept Jesus Christ as truly divine and human.	3. Same.
	4. Practice two ordinances: baptism for converted adults by immersion and the Lord's supper.	4. Believe the sacraments of baptism and the Lord's supper are channels of God's grace for God's people.
	5. Believe the church is composed of believers redeemed through the blood of Christ and commissioned to preach the gospel to all nations.	5. Believe the church is the body of Christ and exists where God's word is preached and the sacraments are rightly administered.
Type of Worship	Free and informal. Nonliturgical with hymn singing, prayers, and scripture reading. Sermon is given prominent place.	Liturgical, following the tradition of the Western church. Both word and sacrament are considered important.
Governance	Resembles presbyterian form, with elders, deacons, and trustees in local congregation. Have District Conferences and annual General Council.	Interdependent congregational, regional, national, and global expressions of the church are characterized by democratic decision making, strong ecumenical relationships, elected leadership, and an ordained ministry.
Statistics	Membership: 428,721 Congregations: 1,978	

CHAPTER 6

CHRISTIAN CHURCH (DISCIPLES OF CHRIST)

Thomas Campbell, an early leader of the Christian Church, traveled on horseback to preach in homes and in outdoor settings.

The Christian Church (Disciples of Christ) is one of the younger church bodies in the world and is typically American in its origin and outlook. It began on the frontier in the early nineteenth century, growing out of a desire for freedom from religious traditions and an impulse for Christian unity.

Freedom and unity are themes that flow through the entire history of the Christian Church (Disciples of Christ). An early leader was Thomas Campbell (1763–1854), a Seceder Presbyterian minister who came to the United States from Ireland in 1807 and was assigned a parish in western Pennsylvania. People who came to him were not all from the same branch of Presbyterianism, yet to him, they were all one people needing his ministry. Leaders of the regional church body did not see his responsibility in this way, and he was soon a minister without a parish.

Disciples of Christ

In reaction to his dismissal, Campbell began a reform program emphasizing the need for Christian unity based on the word of God. Soon the Christian Association of Washington, Pennsylvania, was formed. The Disciples of Christ developed out of this movement. When the Christian Association needed a rationale for its work, Campbell prepared a fifty-six-page document called the *Declaration and Address of the Christian Association of Washington.* It is now one of the basic historical documents of the Christian Church (Disciples of Christ).

The members of the Association thought they could best witness to Christian unity not by fighting within established denominations, but by forming a separate congregation. A journal called *The Christian Baptist,* edited by Campbell, had a tremendous influence on the American frontier. It carried on a crusade against authoritarian creeds, the professional clergy, missionary societies, and ecclesiasticism. It also advocated a restoration of apostolic Christianity as a solid basis on which all churches could unite. This was understood as the task of a new reformation.

Soon there were reformers in many Baptist congregations. Some of these churches remained loyal to Baptist tradition, a few divided, and still others dissolved as Baptist bodies to embrace the new unity movement.

Christian Churches

Even before Campbell started to work among the Baptists, other expressions of the freedom movement appeared in American church life. Christian Churches were established in New England. Several ministers broke with the Methodists over the matter of ecclesiastical authority and formed the Republican Methodist Church, which soon adopted the name Christian Church. The strongest Christian Church group, however, was one that originated in Kentucky. A Presbyterian minister who had participated in a revival with ministers of many faiths was censured, along with other ministers. This led them to form independent and "free" Christian Church groups.

These Christian Church groups, because they were advocating the same principles—freedom, Christian unity, and congregational autonomy—discovered one another and joined forces. They viewed formal creeds as divisive and ecclesiasticism as oppressive, and advocated liberty and Christian unity.

The views of these groups were similar to those of the Baptist reformers, the Disciples of Christ group. Differences between the two movements were more a matter of emphasis than doctrine. The "reformers" focused on restoration of early Christianity and church unity; the "Christians" stressed liberty and freedom. In the 1830s the two bodies united, both at a leadership level and congregation by congregation. The name Christian Church (Disciples of Christ) was chosen and is used today.

Theological Approach

Until recently, members of the church had little interest in theology as such. In general the churches followed the view of Alexander Campbell, who said, "Let the Bible be substituted for all human creed." Because they were advocating simple evangelical Christianity, members of these churches had no interest in analyzing the nature of God, though they affirmed belief in God the Father, Son, and Holy Spirit.

On theological issues such as sin and salvation, the divinity of Christ, the virgin birth, the bodily resurrection, and the second coming of the Lord, there is no more divergence of views than can be found within any other single denomination. Peter's profession of faith in Matthew 16:16 and the Reformation principle of the priesthood of all believers are accepted doctrine in the Christian Church (Disciples of Christ).

Members usually view tradition and creeds with caution. Rather, they look at the Bible for answers to theological questions. The gospel proclamation and the need for the person to respond are emphasized. Because of its witness for Christian unity, the main emphasis of this religious body has been the visible church. The Christian Church (Disciples of Christ) is concerned with theological education, not on a denominational basis, but on a broad ecumenical basis.

The minister is looked on as the spiritual and administrative leader of the congregation. Each congregation is free to develop its own worship. On occasion ancient liturgies are used, but the minister has the privilege of creating public worship that is relevant to the times and to special situations.

Two Ordinances

The Christian Church (Disciples of Christ) observes two ordinances: the Lord's supper and baptism. The first ordinance is celebrated each Sunday as the center of corporate worship. The second ordinance is administered only to believers and by immersion. Some congregations will accept the baptism of people coming from a denomination where another form of baptism is practiced.

The Lord's supper is understood as a memorial, as fellowship with Christ, and as a channel of God's grace. It is administered by the minister and two laypeople (called elders) who have been selected by the congregation, and distributed by several other selected laypeople (called deacons). Participation is open to all people regardless of denomination on the basis of the individual conscience, with Paul's admonition (1 Corinthians 11:27-29) in mind.

Social Issues

Because congregations are autonomous units, agreement on social issues is obtained by exchange of opinion. The General Assembly regularly formulates views on matters of social import but only as recommendations. Peace with justice is a priority of the General Assembly. This priority is expressed through refugee resettlement efforts, ecumenical service projects, and donations of material aid. The Christian Church (Disciples of Christ) also identify with the social ministries of regional, national, and world councils of churches. Representatives are sent to all ecumenical conferences, and there is sensitivity to the Christian social consciences of other denominations.

Affirming the unity of Christians as their polar star, the Christian Church (Disciples of Christ) resolves, "Where the Scriptures speak, we speak; where the Scriptures are silent, we are silent."

For Discussion

1. How do Disciples of Christ and Lutherans differ regarding the historic structures of the church? How are they similar?

2. Compare attitudes of the Christian Church (Disciples of Christ) and the Evangelical Lutheran Church in America toward church union.

3. Do you think it is appropriate for the church to speak, for instance, on social issues where "the Scriptures are silent"? Why or why not?

For Further Study

· *Disciples at Prayer: The Spirituality of the Christian Church (Disciples of Christ)* by William O. Paulsell (Chalice, 1996)

· *The Faith We Affirm: Basic Beliefs of Disciples of Christ* by Ronald E. Osborn (Chalice, 1986)

· *A Handbook for Today's Disciples in the Christian Church (Disciples of Christ)*, 4th ed., by D. Duane Cummins (Chalice, 2010)

· *Renewing Christian Unity: A Concise History of the Christian Church* by Mark G. Toulouse, Gary Holloway, and Douglas A. Foster (Abilene University Christian Press, 2010)

· Christian Church (Disciples of Christ) website: disciples.org

Table of Comparison

	Christian Church (Disciples of Christ)	Lutherans
Teachings	1. Use human statements of faith for insight, but they are not binding or authoritative. 2. Believe a person's duty to become a Christian involves confession of Jesus as Christ, repentance, and baptism. 3. Deny original sin, but believe the person with free will is accountable to God. 4. Observe holy communion in fellowship as a memorial to Christ and as a channel of God's grace. 5. Advocate Christian unity; believe division in Christ's church is sin.	1. Use creeds, catechisms, and confessions as summaries of scripture's teachings. 2. Proclaim God's gospel, eliciting humankind's response of faith by the power of the Holy Spirit. 3. See original sin as the condition of human nature in need of grace. 4. Celebrate holy communion as Christ's real presence and a means of grace. 5. Increasingly accept fellowship with similar Christian denominations.
Type of Worship	Free to use traditional forms of liturgy or to create forms relevant to the times and specific situations. Communion is celebrated each Lord's day as the focal point of worship.	Liturgical order is followed; eucharist is celebrated with increasing frequency, recognizing the unity of word and sacrament.
Governance	Local churches are autonomous; cooperate with others in missionary and benevolent work; hold international convention; support ecumenical structures.	Interdependent congregational, regional, national, and global expressions of the church are characterized by democratic decision making, strong ecumenical relationships, elected leadership, and an ordained ministry.
Statistics	Membership: 785,776 Congregations: 3,625	

CHAPTER 7

CHURCH OF CHRIST, SCIENTIST

Mary Baker Eddy founded the Church of Christ, Scientist, in 1879 after she was healed of serious injuries while reading a story of healing from Matthew.

Christian Science is a worldwide religion based on the Bible, particularly on the teachings and healings of Christ Jesus. A New England woman, Mary Baker Eddy, is the author of the Christian Science textbook, *Science and Health with Key to the Scriptures*, first published in 1875. Eddy saw Christian Science as the law of God, the law of good, that operates universally for the benefit of everyone. *Science and Health* is studied by Christian Scientists, as well as by those of other faiths, in order to better understand the spiritual meaning of the Bible.

God is defined not only as the infinite and eternal Being revealed to Moses as "I AM," and as the healing and sustaining power known to Jesus by the intimate name of Father, but also as Mind, Spirit, Truth, Life, Soul, Principle, Love—terms used or implied in the Bible and set forth explicitly in *Science and Health* as synonyms of Deity. God is also understood as Father-Mother, the creative Principle, the source of all that is perfect, indestructible, and immortal. The creation described in the first chapter of Genesis as both wonderfully fresh and flawlessly complete is identified in Christian Science as the true creation, inherently good and forever spiritual. All evil and suffering are seen as the result of misunderstanding or ignorance of God.

The True Idea of God

The saving Christ or Son of God is explained as the true idea of God—the divine idea embodied in the life of the historic Jesus and shining through his virgin birth, his healing and teaching ministry, his resurrection following the crucifixion, and his final ascension beyond all material limitations. It is his perfect exemplification of the Christ that makes Jesus' life the way of salvation, the supreme model for all humanity. But as Christian Scientists understand it, the Christ-power is by no means confined to the person of Jesus, as he himself indicated when he said, "The one who believes in me will also do the works that I do" (John 14:12). The idea of God must necessarily include the right understanding of true, individual identity as God's image and likeness—spiritual, not material; perfect, not fallen. This understanding rescues and reforms us from sin through revealing each individual's true nature—what it means practically, here and now, to be "heirs of God and joint heirs with Christ" (Romans 8:17). As Christian Scientists see it, this understanding is the Holy Spirit, "the Spirit of truth" that Jesus promised would guide "into all the truth" (John 16:13).

How does one gain this Spirit? Through prayer, grace, study, practice—through grasping the spiritual reality beyond material appearances. This enables one, in Paul's words to the Colossians, to take off the "old self" and put on the "new self," whom Christian Science describes as the only real person. This real person, free from sin, disease, and death, has been humanly demonstrated in full perfection only by Christ Jesus, but remains to be demonstrated by all people in proportion to their understanding of Christ's theology and their obedience to Christ's ethics.

As in the New Testament narratives, spiritual healing is viewed in Christian Science as a central aspect of Christian salvation. It is not, however, considered miraculous or a matter of blind faith, but the natural result of coming into a more understanding communion with God. Of course, the healing of disease is only a part of the total work to be done. All the sorrow, poverty, crime, injustice, fear, pride, and materialism of human life demand healing. The primary task of the individual, as Christian Science sees it, is to know God, to know oneself as his image, to yield to the Christ-spirit that heals what is unlike God, and increasingly to bring this spiritual understanding to bear on the ills of the world.

Students and Practitioners

A Christian Scientist is apt to speak of himself or herself as a *student* of Christian Science. Like the related word *disciple*, the term implies that Christianity is a study, a discipline, as well as a way of life—a devotion of the heart and soul and mind to understanding God as the very source of one's being.

A Christian Scientist may also be thought of as a *practitioner* of Christian Science. Like the term *minister*, the word suggests that Christianity is a practical ministry, a life of service to humanity—the actual practice of Christian insights in daily life. While the term *Christian Science practitioner* is usually reserved for those who give their full time to the public spiritual healing ministry, every student of Christian Science is expected in a measure to be a practitioner of the faith he or she professes.

Worship and Study

Founded by Mary Baker Eddy, the Church of Christ, Scientist, is a lay church. Sunday worship services consist of hymns, silent prayer followed by the Lord's Prayer, and a lesson-sermon composed of passages on selected topics from the Bible and *Science and Health*. This Bible lesson is studied during the preceding week by Christian Scientists throughout the world and is read to the congregation on Sunday by two readers who have been elected for this purpose by, and from, the members of each church. A meeting held on Wednesday evenings includes testimonies of Christian Science healing by members of the congregation, because sharing the fruits of spiritual experience is thought to be very important. In Christian Science Sunday schools, young people learn the relevance of the Bible to their daily lives. Other resources and activities provided by Church of Christ, Scientist, congregations for their communities include reading rooms and public lectures on Christian Science.

The Church of Christ, Scientist, is involved in a variety of ecumenical discussions at local and national levels and worldwide.

For Discussion

1. What do you think of Christian Science teachings on healing, in light of Jesus' healing miracles and today's medical science?

2. What do you think about the statement "All evil and suffering are seen as the result of misunderstanding or ignorance of God"?

3. Lutheran theology teaches that the old, sinful self is very real; Christian Science would disagree. What do you believe, and why?

For Further Study

The following books are available at Christian Science Reading Rooms and public libraries:

· *Healing Spiritually: Renewing Your Life through the Power of God's Law* by Mary Baker Eddy (Christian Science Publishing Society, 1996)

· *Mary Baker Eddy: Christian Healer* by Yvonne Cache von Fettweis and Robert Townsend Warneck (Christian Science Publishing Society, 2009)

· *Science and Health with Key to the Scriptures* by Mary Baker Eddy (Christian Science Board of Directors, 1994)

· Christian Scientist websites:
  - Christian Science: christianscience.com
  - Mary Baker Eddy: www.marybakereddylibrary.org

Table of Comparison

	Christian Scientists	*Lutherans*
Teachings	1. Accept the Bible and *Science and Health with Key to the Scriptures* by Mary Baker Eddy as their textbooks and pastor. 2. Understand the three aspects of the Trinity as God, the Father-Mother; the Son, one Christ; and the Holy Ghost or divine comforter. 3. Believe sin, sickness, and death result from ignorance or misunderstanding of God, and that these are overcome through a right understanding of God. 4. Believe God's creation is wholly spiritual and good.	1. Accept the Bible as the written witness to God's revelation of saving action through Jesus Christ. 2. Maintain classic doctrine of triune God: Father, Son, and Holy Spirit. 3. Believe in the reality of sin, with sickness and death present because of evil. 4. Believe in the reality of God's creation; affirm humankind's creative responsibility within creation.
Type of Worship	A Sunday service consisting of hymns, prayers, and a lesson-sermon comprised of selections from the Bible and *Science and Health* read by two lay readers. A Wednesday evening meeting that includes testimonies of Christian Science healing.	Liturgical patterns of worship used, led by an ordained minister, with preaching of the word and celebration of sacraments involving elements of water, bread, and wine.
Governance	Organized under the *Church Manual* by Mary Baker Eddy, composed of the First Church of Christ, Scientist, in Boston (the mother church), together with local, democratically governed branch Churches of Christ, Scientist, worldwide.	Interdependent congregational, regional, national, and global expressions of the church are characterized by democratic decision making, strong ecumenical relationships, elected leadership, and an ordained ministry.
Statistics	Membership: In accordance with the church's governing documents, no membership statistics are reported for publication. Various scholars estimate membership is under 100,000. Congregations: 1,153	

CHAPTER 8

CHURCH OF GOD

Teachings from the New Testament provide the standard of faith and life for individuals in the Church of God.

More than a million Americans are associated with a Church of God group of some kind. Most of these groups (some two hundred independent bodies) have little in common with each other, however, except for their use of a New Testament name for the church. Almost all are relatively young bodies with recent American origins, frequently with an emphasis on the work of the Holy Spirit to empower and guide people.

This movement has a concern for Christian unity, holy living, and the use of the New Testament as the standard of faith and life. It grew out of a belief that the church was too restricted and burdened by organization and should be more directly under the "rule of God."

The church is seen as the body of Christ on earth. Baptism of believers by immersion, communion, and foot washing are understood to be simply reminders or object lessons about how God works with people. Churches of God have no written creed, but have generally sought to be guided by consensus about the clear teachings of the Bible. This has left much to individual interpretation and has produced personalized faith. Worship practices vary a great deal from congregation to congregation and even from service to service. There is no established liturgy, but worship is carried out with varying degrees of formality.

A unique characteristic of this movement is its attitude toward formal church membership. Out of a belief that only Christ can accept people into the spiritual body of the church, Church of God congregations maintain no formal membership rolls. Followers believe that only when people commit themselves to Christ do they become a part of the church. Someone is considered a member in God's judgment only.

For Discussion

1. In general, Churches of God have stressed the work of the Holy Spirit, and Lutherans have stressed the work of Jesus Christ. How do you think these different emphases may have shaped the denominations?

2. What are the benefits and drawbacks of the Church of God approach to membership?

For Further Study

· *The Church of God: A Social History* by Mickey Crews (University of Tennessee Press, 1990)

· *Like a Mighty Army: A History of the Church of God, 1886–1995* (Pathway, 1995)

· Websites
  - Church of God (Cleveland, Tennessee): www.churchofgod.org
  - Church of God (Anderson, Indiana): www.jesusisthesubject.org
  - Church of God in Christ (Memphis, Tennessee): www.cogic.com
  - Church of God in Christ, Mennonite: churchofgodinchristmennonite.net

Note: There is no comparison table for this chapter because Church of God groups vary in their teachings, type of worship, and governance.

Statistics*   Membership: 2,245,214
                    Congregations: 14,602

*More than two hundred bodies bear the name Church of God. Figures are based on eight denominations.

CHAPTER 9

THE CHURCH OF JESUS CHRIST OF LATTER-DAY SAINTS

Following the murder of their prophet, Joseph Smith, in 1844, the Latter-day Saints traveled west from Illinois to what is now Utah.

The Church of Jesus Christ of Latter-day Saints, sometimes referred to by the unofficial name Mormon Church, is a worldwide church with a total membership of approximately fifteen million. Organized at Fayette, New York, on April 6, 1830, the church is not an offshoot of another church body but claims to be a restoration of the Church of Jesus Christ, established by Jesus of Nazareth when he lived on the earth.

Continuing Revelations

The Latter-day Saints believe that both the Old and New Testaments contain the word of God and profess to have the same church organization as the primitive church. They believe that revelations were given and will continue to be given to all people who seek God. Joseph Smith, founder of the church, published *The Book of Mormon* in 1830. It is said to contain a translation of ancient records. *The Doctrine and Covenants* (1835) contains revelations given to Smith with additions from his successors. Another book, *The Pearl of Great Price* (1851), is a selection of materials from the revelations, translations, and narrations of Smith, including the Articles of Faith, a brief statement of principal doctrines of the church. Because of the nature of its origins and its claim to divine authority, the church does not join ecumenical movements.

Seeking a New Zion

This church, after its organization in New York state, was persecuted by its neighbors, causing the group to move to Ohio in 1831. Desiring to set up a new Zion, most of the members moved westward from Ohio to Missouri during the years 1831 to 1838. Conflict over the slavery issue (the members were largely from New England), cooperative buying and selling, and various religious beliefs led to mob uprisings that resulted in the "Saints," as they were called, being driven from Missouri, a slave state. The fleeing church members were welcome in Illinois, where between 1839 and 1846 they built the prosperous city of Nauvoo, for a time the largest city in that state.

Following the murder of their prophet, Joseph Smith, and his brother Hyrum by a mob in 1844, the church's members again turned westward. Some sixteen thousand members spent the winter of 1846 to 1847 on the western plains. In 1847 the advance companies of the exiles traveled eleven hundred miles across plain and desert and settled in the Great Basin, centering at what is now Salt Lake City.

During the next thirty years, under the leadership of Brigham Young, 375 colonies were established in the western Rocky Mountain area—the beginnings of many of the cities now there. The first civil government was known as the Provisional State of Deseret (1849–51). Utah was organized as a United States territory in 1850 and continued as a territory until 1896, when statehood was achieved.

Emphasis on Education

The Latter-day Saints organized schools wherever they went. What is now the University of Utah was established by the church as the University of Deseret in 1850. Latter-day Saint educators may be found in nearly every major higher learning institution in the United States.

Committed to a philosophy that real education requires instruction in both secular and religious subjects, the Latter-day Saints have seminaries adjacent to public high schools, and Institutes of Religion adjacent to colleges and universities, where students may supplement secular education with religious instruction.

God and Humankind

Members of the Church of Jesus Christ of Latter-day Saints believe that people are created in the image of God and that God is a being with a body and passions, a supreme being separate from the bodily form of Jesus Christ, who is literally the Son of God.

They accept the biblical account of Jesus Christ as found in the Gospels, the Letters, and other writings of the New Testament. These present Jesus as the literal Son of God in the flesh, teaching the perfect gospel, being in frequent communication with his Father during his ministry, performing mighty miracles, dying on the cross to save humankind, and rising from the dead with his actual body of flesh and bones, which he showed to many disciples.

The Latter-day Saints believe that the Holy Ghost, or Holy Spirit, is a being without body through whom the Father and the Son may communicate with humankind and achieve the work of the Godhead. The Latter-day Saints claim that additional teachings of the Christ were found in America on ancient gold plates and translated into English by Joseph Smith. This account is published as *The Book of Mormon* and has a circulation exceeding ninety million copies.

This church believes that humankind is eternal, that people are the literal offspring of God, and that people existed in spiritual bodies before life on earth and will live again in the spirit world and eventually be resurrected with a body of flesh and bone. Humankind may progress eternally and may become as the gods. Marriage, when performed by the priesthood in sacred temples of the church, continues beyond this life.

Church Organization

The Church of Jesus Christ of Latter-day Saints is founded on authority claimed to have been received directly from the resurrected Christ through divine messengers: John the Baptist, Peter, James, and John, as well as the ancient prophets Moses, Elias, and Elijah. Through this priesthood authority the church was organized and is governed.

The priesthood is held in varying degrees by most of the male members of the church twelve years of age and older, who constitute a vast body of volunteer workers. Women have equal sustaining vote (members' formal vote to endorse certain leadership decisions) in the church and serve as teachers and officers in the Relief Society auxiliary, Primary (the children's organization and official auxiliary), Sunday school, and the Young Women organization for teenage girls.

A prophet heads this church with counselors, the Quorum of the Twelve Apostles, the Quorums of the Seventy, and the Presiding Bishopric. These constitute what is known as the General Authorities.

The church is divided into ecclesiastical and geographical divisions called *stakes*, each presided over by three high priests and a high council of twelve (all unpaid lay members). Each stake is divided into geographic wards, usually five or more. Each ward is presided over by a bishop and two counselors to the bishop, with one or more ward clerks. All are lay members and receive no salary.

Baptism and Meeting

People become members of this church through baptism by immersion by one holding priesthood authority. Children are baptized when they reach the age of accountability, defined as the age of eight. Following baptism, the Holy Ghost is conferred by the laying on of hands by those holding the Melchizedek Priesthood.

The principal worship service, a sacrament meeting, is held each Sunday. There priests or elders of the church bless the emblems of the sacrament, bread and water, and administer them to the members.

Missionary Work

The Church of Jeus Christ of Latter-day Saints is concerned with every aspect of life and carries on an elaborate program to foster health, recreation, care of people who are poor, education, the arts, and the general welfare of its members. It maintains strict separation of church and state, but urges members to participate in the civic and political processes of their nation.

Some 330 missions cover most of the globe. About sixty thousand missionaries are kept in these missions, serving at their own expense for an average of twenty-four months. Other missionaries serve on a part-time basis in the various stakes of the church. The missionary zeal accounts for much of the growth in church membership.

For Discussion

1. In many instances, the beliefs of Latter-day Saints are similar to historic Christian teachings, but with some variation. Find examples of this, and reflect on the significance of the differences.

2. How do you think the American beginnings of the Church of Jesus Christ of Latter-day Saints have helped, and hindered, its growth?

3. A historical comparison can be made between the Church of Jesus Christ of Latter-day Saints and Islam. What similarities and differences can you see in their development?

For Further Study

- *A Different Jesus? The Christ of the Latter-day Saints* by Robert L. Millet (Eerdmans, 2005)

- *The Encyclopedia of Mormonism* (Macmillan, 1992), 4 vols., available in many libraries

- *Mormonism Explained: What Latter-day Saints Teach and Practice* by Andrew Jackson (Crossway, 2008)

- Latter-day Saints website: www.lds.org

Table of Comparison

	Latter-day Saints	Lutherans
Teachings	1. Believe in God, the Eternal Father; Jesus Christ, God's Son; and the Holy Ghost. These three are considered separate personages but one in purpose.	1. Confess the unity of the triune God: Father, Son, and Holy Spirit.
	2. Believe the Bible to be the word of God. Also believe *The Book of Mormon*. Accept revelations received by the prophets of the present Latter-day Saints.	2. Believe the Bible is the written witness to God's revelation of saving action through Jesus Christ. Christ is the great revelation of God; revelations contrary to Christ are rejected.
	3. Believe revelation has not ceased; new ones may come at any time.	3. Believe the New Testament faith was "once for all delivered."
	4. Reject original sin. Children are considered to be born innocent and cannot sin until they understand right from wrong.	4. Believe all people are born under bondage to evil; the power of God's grace is needed to free humankind from this captivity.
	5. Reject infant baptism, since children are believed to be without sin. Practice baptism for the dead. Immersion only, by one holding authority.	5. Baptize infants. Do not reject any method of baptism. Baptism for the dead is seen as contrary to scripture.
	6. Consider communion a symbol, a renewing of covenants with Christ. Use the emblems of bread and water.	6. Affirm the real presence of Christ in the sacrament of holy communion. Use the elements of bread and wine.
Type of Worship	No liturgy. Communion is celebrated every Sunday. No formally trained or paid ministry to lead the service.	Liturgical pattern of worship is used with holy communion celebrated regularly. Ordained ministry.
Governance	Centralized and hierarchical structure. Governance at all levels is deliberated in consultative councils. Decisions on important matters must be unanimous.	Interdependent congregational, regional, national, and global expressions of the church are characterized by democratic decision making, strong ecumenical relationships, elected leadership, and an ordained ministry.
Statistics	Membership: 6,144,582 Congregations: 13,601	

CHAPTER 10

CHURCH OF THE BRETHREN

The love feast or communion service (an ordinance in Church of the Brethren) includes a foot washing ceremony symbolizing servanthood.

The Church of the Brethren is one of the older denominations in the Believers Church or Free Church tradition. Originating in 1708 as a separatist movement among German Pietists, Brethren were strongly influenced by Anabaptism (see the chapter on the Mennonite Church). By 1735 the Brethren had migrated from Germany to colonial America, where they were often called "Dunkers" because of their distinctive practice of baptizing adult believers by threefold immersion. Their Germanic culture, strict social ethic, and pacifist convictions kept them isolated from mainstream American life until the latter half of the nineteenth century. By that time they had expanded to the West Coast, with no congregations, however, in New England and few in the Deep South.

Brethren accept the Bible as the trustworthy word of God to which they teach obedience. Most Brethren take the New Testament as a higher and more complete revelation than the Old Testament, while still affirming the unity of the scriptures.

Brethren accept the basic tenets of Protestant Christianity but are not creedal in a strict sense. They do on occasion use the traditional creeds as affirmations of faith.

Church practices are usually referred to as *ordinances* (commandments of the Lord) rather than sacraments. They include baptism by immersion, a love feast or communion (with foot washing after John 13:3-17, a fellowship meal, and the eucharist), and anointing for spiritual and bodily health.

Brethren have been active in higher education, publishing, and world missions. Former mission congregations in India, China, Nigeria, and Ecuador have become independent bodies related to national churches. Brethren have been particularly known for a worldwide program of social welfare, relief and reconstruction, and peace activities. Although Brethren teach Christian pacifism, members who enter the military service remain in good standing. The Church of the Brethren is a member of the National and World Councils of Churches.

For Discussion

1. How do you think the old nickname "Dunkers" reflects common attitudes toward faith traditions we don't understand?

2. Would you argue that it is wise or unwise for Christians to keep somewhat separate from certain aspects of society? Why?

For Further Study

· *Against the Wind: Eberhard Arnold and the Bruderhof* by Markus Baum and Jim Wallis (Plough, 1998)

· *Meet the Brethren*, ed. Donald F. Durnbaugh (Brethren, 1984)

· *Portrait of a People: The Church of the Brethren at 300* by Carl Bowman (Brethren, 2008)

· Church of the Brethren website: www.brethren.org

Table of Comparison

	Brethren	Lutherans
Teachings	1. Believe the Bible is the trustworthy word of God.	1. Accept the Bible as the written witness to God's revelation of saving action through Jesus Christ.
	2. Believe in the triune nature of God.	2. Same.
	3. Believe in the full divinity and full humanity of Christ.	3. Same.
	4. Accept the creeds as nonbinding affirmations of faith.	4. Subscribe to the ecumenical creeds: Apostles', Nicene, and Athanasian.
	5. Practice the ordinances of believer's baptism; love feast, including foot washing, meal, and communion; and anointing.	5. Celebrate two sacraments: baptism, including that of infants, and holy communion.
	6. Teach Christian pacifism.	6. Value peacemaking, but pacifism is not taught as a basic Christian position.
Type of Worship	A mixture of "low church" and more liturgical norms.	Liturgical, following the primary pattern of the Western church.
Governance	Combination of congregational and Presbyterian polity.	Interdependent congregational, regional, national, and global expressions of the church are characterized by democratic decision making, strong ecumenical relationships, elected leadership, and an ordained ministry.
Statistics	Membership: 146,588 Congregations: 1,032	

CHAPTER 11

CHURCH OF THE NAZARENE

Trained evangelists who go door to door help the Church of the Nazarene grow.

The Church of the Nazarene started on October 8, 1908, when three holiness groups from the East, the West, and the South united. This merger culminated a movement that began in the nineteenth century to conserve and spread the doctrine of holiness.

Strongly biblical in emphasis, the Church of the Nazarene is Wesleyan-Arminian in theology. Therefore, the doctrine of entire sanctification, which teaches that the Christian may be cleansed from inborn sin, is particularly significant to the denomination. Everyone is believed to be born with a nature averse to God and inclined toward evil. The Holy Spirit makes people aware of their sin and provides *prevenient* grace (grace in anticipation of repentance) that enables them to turn from their sin in repentance and have faith in Christ. This conversion experience is the beginning of the Christian life. It is followed by spiritual growth. At some point in the Christian pilgrimage, every believer realizes that even though God has forgiven his or her sins, there remains an inner inclination toward evil. The Holy Spirit draws the Christian to commit his or her life completely to God. When Christians respond in faith to this call to consecration, they are entirely sanctified. This means they are cleansed from the inclination toward evil and are "perfected in love" for God.

The whole Christian church is said to include all spiritually regenerate people. Members of the Church of the Nazarene voluntarily come together and follow the doctrine and polity of the denomination. Members are admitted on the basis of their confession of faith and their agreement to submit to the church's government.

Two ordinances are observed: baptism by sprinkling, pouring, or most often immersion, and the Lord's supper. Baptism is administered to believers as a sign of their faith in Christ and their intent to follow Christ. Young children may be baptized on the request of parents who promise to provide for their Christian training.

The Lord's supper is considered a memorial of Christ's sacrificial death. It is only for those who have faith in Christ and are living the Christian life. Communicants receive both the unleavened bread and the nonfermented wine.

Traditionally, worship in the church has been characterized by freedom and personal involvement. Both music and preaching play important roles in worship services.

For Discussion

1. What do you think of the idea that Christians can become completely sanctified—perfected in love—in this life?
2. The Nazarene practice of baptism seems to be a mix of infant baptism and believer's baptism. Compare the theology behind this with that of your church's baptismal practice.

For Further Study

· *Our Watchword and Song: The Centennial History of the Church of the Nazarene* by Floyd Cunningham (Beacon Hill, 2009)
· *Welcome to the Church of the Nazarene* by Richard Leslie Parrott (Beacon Hill, 1988)
· Church of the Nazarene website: nazarene.org

Table of Comparison

	Nazarenes	Lutherans
Teachings	1. Believe original sin may be cleansed in the work of entire sanctification. This work of grace is after regeneration and is possible in this life.	1. Believe Christian life is growth in forgiveness, but perfection is never completed in this life.
	2. Believe all spiritually regenerate persons are members of the church.	2. Teach that the church exists where God's word is preached and the sacraments are rightly administered.
	3. Consider baptism and the Lord's supper to be signs of faith.	3. Believe the sacraments of baptism and Lord's supper are means of grace and affirm the real presence of Christ in communion.
	4. See the Bible as the divinely inspired word of God.	4. Believe the Bible is the written witness to God's revelation of saving action through Jesus Christ.
	5. Believe in the triune nature of God as well as the full divinity and humanity of Christ.	5. Same.
	6. Believe salvation is possible only through personal faith in the atonement for sin made by Jesus Christ.	6. Teach salvation by grace through faith apart from works of the law.
Type of Worship	Characterized by freedom and personal involvement. Emphasis on preaching with strong evangelism.	Liturgical, following the Western pattern, with both the preaching of the gospel and the celebration of the sacraments considered important.
Governance	Representative in form; local congregation selects pastor and manages own affairs. Governing boards elected by supervising group.	Interdependent congregational, regional, national, and global expressions of the church are characterized by democratic decision making, strong ecumenical relationships, elected leadership, and an ordained ministry.
Statistics	Membership: 893,649 Congregations: 5,056	

CHAPTER 12

EASTERN ORTHODOX CHURCH

In the Eastern church, the sacrament of holy communion is administered by a spoon from a chalice where the leavened bread and wine have been mixed together.

The word *orthodox*, meaning "true belief," was given to the Eastern church because of its efforts in the early days of Christianity to preserve the true faith of Christ. When the Christian faith was challenged by false teachers, the Eastern church called the first seven ecumenical councils that defined and explained some of the basic beliefs of Christianity. Major decrees of these councils accepted by Orthodox Christians today include the divinity of Christ, the two natures of Christ (divine and human, united in one person), and the Nicene Creed, which is the official creed of the Eastern Orthodox Church.

Eastern Orthodoxy made an atypical entrance into North America. Although most immigrants came first to the East Coast and gradually moved westward, Eastern Orthodoxy traveled in the opposite direction. Russian Orthodox missionaries established a mission in 1794 on Kodiak Island off the coast of Alaska. When the United States purchased that territory from Russia, these Orthodox missionaries spread their work from Alaska as far south as San Francisco. Later they moved their work to Minneapolis, where they started a seminary, and from there Orthodox Christians went eastward to Pennsylvania, New York, and other states.

Worldwide, the Eastern church constitutes the third largest body of Christians, with approximately 170 million Orthodox Christians. There are three main groups of Eastern Christians: (1) the *Eastern Orthodox*, such as the Greek and Russian churches; (2) the *Oriental Orthodox*, such as the Copts and the Armenians, who separated from the Byzantine Orthodox in the fifth century for ethnic and theological reasons; and (3) the *Greek Catholic* or Uniate churches, such as the Melchites and Maronites, which are in union with Rome. This chapter presents the first group, the Eastern Orthodox Church, a family of thirteen self-governing bodies, including Syrian, Greek, Ukrainian, Russian, Bulgarian, Serbian, Romanian, and Albanian churches.

From the Apostles

The Eastern Orthodox Church dates its existence from the time of the apostles. The apostle Paul, for example, established the Christian church in Greece through his early missionary journeys. The apostle Peter founded the church in Antioch. Other apostles established churches in Jerusalem, Alexandria, and Cyprus. From these cities and countries, missionaries brought the gospel of Christ to many other countries.

Although Eastern Orthodox churches govern themselves independently and use their own languages in the liturgy, they share the same beliefs, worship service, and sacraments. The patriarch of Constantinople is recognized by all Eastern Orthodox churches as the spiritual head of the church in *honor* only. He has no authority comparable to that of the pope.

English is replacing the many foreign languages used in the liturgy by the approximately four million Orthodox Christians in the United States. Although the various Orthodox churches in America still govern themselves independently, they cooperate in religious education, campus ministry, and chaplaincy work.

Worship with Joy

The Eastern Orthodox Church has always placed great emphasis on worship, and its services last longer than services of most Christian churches in the West. Its main worship service—the liturgy—has captured the element of sheer joy in the resurrection of Jesus that is found in the writings of the early church.

The liturgy is important in Eastern Orthodoxy because it is the means by which a person communes with the Lord Jesus. In the first part of the liturgy, the Eastern Christian communes with Christ as the Word of God. This section primarily consists of readings from the holy scriptures followed by an explanation of them in the sermon, an important element of the liturgy. Through the scripture lessons and the sermon, Christ himself speaks to the people. A personal encounter with the living Christ occurs.

In the second part of the liturgy, worshipers commune with Christ as the bread of life. They receive the body and blood of Jesus through the sacrament of holy communion. Both communions—the encounter with Christ as the Word and Christ as the bread of life—are ways of partaking of Christ. Both are achieved through the liturgy as it is celebrated every Sunday and on major feast days.

Orthodox worship services appeal to the whole person through the five senses: *sight*, through the visual beauty of icons (religious paintings) and vestments; *smell*, through the use of incense; *sound*, through the music of the Orthodox liturgy; *taste*, through the sacrament of holy communion and drinking of holy water; and *touch*, by crossing oneself, kissing the icon, and lighting candles on entering an Orthodox church.

Seven Mysteries

The word for *sacrament* in Greek is *mysterion*, meaning "mystery." The word *mystery* expresses a fundamental characteristic of the Orthodox Church: its emphasis on the mystery of God. No attempt is made to define what is indefinable in God. Seven "mysteries" or sacraments are practiced in the Orthodox Church, together with sacramentals, or lesser sacraments. The blessing of holy water and the practice of tonsure (shaving heads) of monks are examples of sacramentals.

Applied to the sacraments, the word *mystery* denotes the mysterious way God brings grace and love to us through these channels. The seven sacraments include the following:

· *Communion.* In the Eastern church, the sacrament of holy communion is administered by a spoon from a chalice where the leavened bread and wine have been mixed together.

   Just as the Orthodox Church does not attempt to define God, it accepts the mystery of what happens to the bread and wine in holy communion without trying to define how it happens. The word *transubstantiation* is used, but it is one of many terms employed to describe the change. The Orthodox insist, however, that the bread and wine become the true body and blood of Jesus Christ.

- *Baptism.* The sacrament of baptism is administered in infancy by the total immersion of the naked infant in the baptismal font. This is done in the name of the holy Trinity. Orthodox Christians usually wear a small cross as a reminder of their baptism.

- *Confirmation.* The sacrament of confirmation is administered immediately following baptism. The newly baptized and confirmed infant becomes a full member of the church and begins to receive holy communion from the time of baptism.

- *Confession.* The sacrament of confession takes the form of a private conference between the priest and the penitent. The penitent kneels before an icon of the Savior. The priest, standing behind or beside the penitent, also faces the icon. This positioning emphasizes that it is not the priest, but God who is the judge. After the penitent makes his or her confession to Christ, the priest pronounces Christ's forgiveness on the penitent.

- *Holy unction.* The sacrament of holy unction is conferred on any person who is sick. This sacrament consists of prayer and the anointing of the sick person with consecrated oil.

- *Holy orders.* The sacrament of holy orders is performed by the bishop. The three major orders in the Orthodox Church are bishop, priest, and deacon. Priests and deacons may be either married or unmarried. If they are to be married, they must choose the state of marriage before ordination. Marriage is not permitted after ordination. Bishops are elected only from the unmarried clergy.

- *Matrimony.* In the sacrament of holy matrimony the couple receives Christ's blessing. Like the five wise maidens in the Bible, the bride and groom hold candles throughout the ceremony to express their eagerness to receive Christ the bridegroom as he comes to bless them through this sacrament. They drink wine from the same cup, signifying that they will share everything in life. They also are crowned with a crown of leaves or one of silver and gold to emphasize the special grace of the Holy Spirit who "crowns" them with glory and honor as king and queen of their small kingdom, their home.

Orthodox Customs

Worshipers receive the *Antidoron*, a little piece of bread, from the priest at the conclusion of each liturgy. This bread is blessed but not consecrated, although taken from the loaf used in the consecration. In many Orthodox parishes, non-Orthodox people present at the liturgy are encouraged to receive the Antidoron as an expression of Christian fellowship and love.

Some Orthodox churches, notably the Russian, Ukrainian, Serbian, and Bulgarian, observe Christmas on January 7 because they still follow the old Julian calendar. The Greek, Syrian, and Romanian churches, having adopted the Gregorian calendar, celebrate Christmas on December 25.

The date of Easter also rarely coincides with that of the West. Usually it occurs a week or more later. This practice stems from the Eastern Orthodox interpretation of scripture in which the resurrection of Jesus is believed to have occurred *following* the Jewish Passover.

Icons

The Eastern church makes extensive use of icons—religious paintings of Christ and the saints. During the early history of the church, the iconoclasts (icon breakers) set out to destroy all icons. They believed that it was idolatrous to paint a picture of God, who is eternal and invisible. The Orthodox Christians, on the other hand, insisted that God could be painted because God had become a person in Jesus.

Icons have been called prayers, hymns, and sermons in form and color. They are the visual gospel. Orthodox Christians use icons in their homes as a reminder of God's presence and for family prayer. In an Orthodox church, the faithful may see unfolded before them almost all the mysteries of the Christian religion captured in paintings on the walls and ceiling.

The idea of the communion of saints, the saints on earth communing with the saints in heaven, is greatly emphasized in the Eastern church. This communion is expressed effectively in the way icons are arranged in the Orthodox Church. The figure of Christ is painted on the top of the dome. Below that, on the walls and apse (altar area), are painted the members of the church triumphant in heaven—the Virgin Mary, the prophets, the angels, and the apostles. Finally, on the floor level of the church are the living saints, the members of the church militant on earth. Thus, around the figure of Christ in the dome is gathered the entire church, both that in heaven and that on earth. As members of a great body, the Eastern Orthodox do not feel alone when they pray, because the church triumphant is praying with them.

Bible and Tradition

A distinctive feature of the Orthodox Church is its loyalty to tradition. The Eastern church recognizes two sources of faith: scripture and sacred tradition. Sacred tradition does not refer to the tradition of human beings or a slavish attachment to the past, but to a living connection with the entire past of the church. It includes all that the Holy Spirit has taught and continues to teach through the church. More specifically, sacred tradition means the books of the Bible, the Nicene Creed, the decrees of the ecumenical councils, and the writings of the church fathers.

The Orthodox Church considers the Bible to be the supreme expression of God's revelation to humankind. The Bible, therefore, occupies a unique preeminence within sacred tradition. So does the Nicene Creed. These are absolute and cannot be canceled or revised. Other parts of sacred tradition, such as the canons, the service books, and the icons, do not have the same authority and can be changed.

Source of Authority

The highest authority of the Eastern church is the ecumenical council, a meeting involving the whole church. The bishops of all the orthodox churches in the world meet together when necessary to discuss common problems. When the bishops define a matter of faith in an ecumenical council, the church as a whole must accept their decision. Only then can it be considered infallible or inspired of the Holy Spirit, who resides in the whole church, consisting of clergy and laity, to guide it to all truth. This makes every person within the church responsible for Christian truth.

Response through Service

Eastern Orthodox Christians believe that the thankful Christian responds to God for what God has done in Christ. This response is *diakonia*—service to one's neighbor. Faith is expressed in deed. As a result of this awareness, the Orthodox Church teaches that personal salvation expresses itself in social concern, inviting the Christian to be a servant to all people for Christ's sake.

For Discussion

1. Even though its liturgy is elaborate and rarely embraces change, the Eastern Orthodox Church has grown rapidly in recent years. Why do you think this might be so?

2. What characteristics of traditional icons catch your eye? Do you think they could aid in your own worship? If so, why?

3. How are your church and Eastern Orthodoxy similar? How are they different?

For Further Study

- *Eastern Orthodox Christianity: A Western Perspective*, 2nd ed., by Daniel B. Clendenin (Baker, 2003)
- *Introducing the Orthodox Church*, 19th ed., by Anthony M. Coniaris and Stephen S. Karakas (Light and Life, 2010)
- *The Orthodox Church* by Timothy Ware (Penguin, 1993)
- *The Orthodox Way* by Kallistos Ware (St. Vladimir's Seminary Press, 1995)
- Websites
  - Orthodox Church in America: www.oca.org
  - Greek Orthodox Archdiocese of America: www.goarch.org

Table of Comparison

	Eastern Orthodox	Lutherans
Teachings	1. Accept the original Nicene Creed, which did not include the filioque phrase.* Orthodox Christians believe that the Holy Spirit proceeds only from the Father and is sent through the Son. 2. Accept the Bible and seven general councils as authority. 3. Celebrate seven sacraments. 4. Believe in transubstantiation, that the bread and wine in communion are changed into the body and blood of Christ. 5. Maintain apostolic succession in that priests must be ordained in an unbroken line back to the apostles.	1. Same, with addition of Western filioque phrase. The Western church believes that the Holy Spirit proceeds from the Father and the Son. 2. Accept the Bible as authority, expressed in creeds and confessions. 3. Celebrate two sacraments: baptism and holy communion. 4. Believe in consubstantiation, that the communicant receives the body and blood of Christ with the bread and wine. 5. Understand apostolic succession as continuity with the apostles' teaching.
Type of Worship	Highly liturgical with Eastern Rite. Usually in the language of the people but not always so.	Liturgical, following the tradition and services of the Western church. Language of the people used.
Governance	An episcopal form of government with bishops, priests, and deacons. Patriarchs and archbishops occupy the more important bishoprics but are not more important in theory.	Interdependent congregational, regional, national, and global expressions of the church are characterized by democratic decision making, strong ecumenical relationships, elected leadership, and an ordained ministry.
Statistics**	Membership: 779,704 Congregations: 1,882	

*Filioque is Latin for "and the Son." Thus, the original, and still the Orthodox version, states in the third article that the Spirit "proceeds from the Father. With the Father and the Son. . . ."

**Figures include ten bodies that are members of the Assembly of Canonical Orthodox Bishops of North and Central America, three of which also have members in Canada and Australia.

CHAPTER 13

EPISCOPAL CHURCH

Henry VIII won permission from Parliament to become the head of the Church of England, thus making it independent of papal control.

People who are not Episcopalians sometimes have difficulty figuring out just what the Episcopal Church is all about. Sometimes Episcopalians seem to be more like Catholics; sometimes they seem not much different from Protestants. Occasionally, they refer to themselves as high church or low church. Even their church buildings reveal differences: one building will be elaborately furnished, while another will look as simple as a New England meetinghouse. Some Episcopal clergy wear colorful vestments; others do not. Why all the variations?

Political in Origin

The Episcopal Church looks the way it does—and believes what it believes, for that matter—because of its history. It came into being as a separate denomination not for theological reasons but for political and jurisdictional ones. According to tradition, the church in England developed from Celtic roots beginning in the first or second century. By the sixth and seventh centuries, it had come under the authority of Rome. It might have remained so, except for several religious and political events in the sixteenth century, during the Protestant Reformation, that can be summed up in two words: *money* and *monarchy*.

Henry VII took over the throne of England in 1485 after a long and bitter civil war, but he did not have a legal right to do so. Fearful of another civil war, his son, King Henry VIII, decided he needed a male heir to make certain his family continued in power. Henry and his wife, Catherine of Aragon, had only a daughter, however, so he asked the pope for an *annulment* (that is, a setting aside) of his marriage. Popes had in the past been willing to grant annulments of royal marriages, particularly when the matter of heirs to the throne came up. But unfortunately, the pope to whom Henry appealed was at the time a political prisoner of the king of Spain, who happened to be Catherine's nephew. The pope, quite understandably, did not wish to offend his captor and refused Henry's request.

Henry adopted a different strategy. In 1534 he won permission from Parliament to become the head of the Church of England, thus making it independent of papal control. Once he had done so, the church granted him the annulment he sought. The king's treasury also benefited from the independence of the church. Large amounts of money that had formerly gone to the pope now went to Henry. The king remarried, and another daughter (the future Elizabeth I) was born to the couple. His second wife, Anne Boleyn, was executed a few years later for treason, and Henry married a third time. Of this marriage, finally, a son was born.

Monarchs and the Church

When Henry VIII died, his ten-year-old son, Edward VI, succeeded him. Under Edward, the Church of England came strongly under the influence of German and Swiss reformers. Edward was only a boy, and his advisers, chief among them Archbishop of Canterbury Thomas Cranmer, were sympathetic to Lutheran and Calvinist ideas. Under Henry's direction the Bible had been translated into English, and parts of the church's services were spoken in English. But under Edward the use of Latin was abolished, and the *Book of Common Prayer* was issued and ordered to be used throughout England. In many parts of that prayer book, one can see evidence of Reformed theology. While Henry was king, few theological changes were made in the beliefs of the Church of England, but during Edward's reign, the influence of the reformers grew. If Edward had reigned for a long time, the Church of England might have developed into a Reformed church.

Edward VI lived only six years after coming to the throne, however. When he died, Henry's older daughter, Mary I, the child of Catherine of Aragon, succeeded him. She was a devout Roman Catholic, and during her reign the Church of England was returned to papal control. Eager to demonstrate her loyalty to the pope, Mary executed Cranmer, the author of the *Book of Common Prayer*, and burned other bishops at the stake. When she died, unhappy and unloved by her subjects, the throne went to Henry's second daughter, Elizabeth I.

Probably because the reigns of her half brother and half sister had been marked by religious intolerance, Elizabeth wanted the Church of England to make room for both Protestants and Catholics. Under the resulting so-called Elizabethan Settlement, the church retained much of its Roman Catholic heritage. Church government, for instance, remained like that of the old days, with bishops, priests, and deacons. A Roman Catholic understanding of the sacraments was retained, but certain concessions were made to the reformers. While fundamental Christian doctrines, such as that of the incarnation, were carefully retained, the Bible and the services were required to be read in English, not Latin. Clergy were allowed to marry.

The Elizabethan Settlement did not ease all hard feelings. Indeed, even today some individuals and groups within the Episcopal Church, like the reformers and the Roman Catholics of Elizabeth's time, would like to see more of one tradition or the other. The church, however, officially retains both Roman Catholic and Protestant elements, as well as vestiges of its original Celtic spirit.

Episcopal Church in America

As English colonists came to America, they brought their church with them. They were Protestant refugees from the religious conflict in England, however, and after the American Revolution, the American branch of the Anglican Church broke its formal ties with the Church of England and became an independent, national church. But like other, similar offshoots (in Canada, Australia, and New Zealand, for instance), the Episcopal Church remains part of the Anglican Communion—that is, the group of national churches sharing the same historical bond and the same understanding of Christianity.

Theology, Scripture, and Tradition

Given its background, it is no wonder that no particular theological label can be applied to the Episcopal Church. But its theology is not much different from that of other Christian bodies. The doctrine of the Trinity—God as Father, Son, and Holy Spirit—is central, and Episcopalians use both the Nicene and the Apostles' Creeds as affirmations of this doctrine. Human beings, according to Anglican belief, were—and are—created free, but they rebelled against their creator. Their rebellion left them isolated and fearful, unable to restore their relationship with God by their own efforts. The incarnation united humanity with God, and the crucifixion and resurrection overcame the power of humanity's rebellious nature. The church does the work of God on earth by continuing the work of Christ. The Episcopal Church looks both to holy scripture and tradition as the means by which we can understand how God's work of salvation is accomplished. Holy scripture, it is agreed, contains everything necessary for Christian belief, but tradition enriches and interprets scripture.

Sacraments are the means by which God unites with humans and helps them live Christian lives in a difficult world. Holy baptism, for instance, gives people a new start. In this sacrament, God breaks the hold of sin on a person and makes the individual a part of the church. Holy communion renews the relationship with God and the church that was given in baptism. Episcopalians believe Christ is present in the bread and wine of the eucharist, but the way in which Christ is present is not considered to be of great importance.

Only these two sacraments, baptism and the eucharist, were ordained by Christ as shown in the scriptures, so the Episcopal Church regards only these two as necessary for salvation. However, Christian tradition, as far back as the apostles' time, has singled out other acts as sacramental. As understood by the Episcopal Church, these sacramental helps are

- *confirmation*, in which a mature Christian renews the vows of baptism in a sort of ordination;
- *reconciliation of a penitent*, or confession of sins in the presence of a priest, who assures the pardon and grace of absolution;
- *ordination*, which confers authority and the grace of the Holy Spirit to those who are to serve God and the church in ordained ministry;
- *holy matrimony*, for those who are being married; and
- *unction of the sick*, which provides God's help for people who are sick or dying.

These five sacramental helps or graces are like the sacraments described in the Bible because they make use of visible signs and actions as channels for God's love and power. These sacramental helps were not commanded by Christ as necessary for the Christian life, however. Rather, they are part of a tradition that forms a portion of the church's life. Many Episcopalians make use of these sacramental helps, but no one is required to do so.

The *Book of Common Prayer*

Worship in the Episcopal Church is based on the *Book of Common Prayer*, although parishes choose which of the options in the prayer book they will use. The central act of worship is the holy eucharist, or holy communion. In most cases, Episcopalian services are liturgical in nature. That is, they follow a more or less fixed form that always includes congregational participation. The liturgy may be enriched with additional prayers, ceremonies, and music; alternatively, the form may be kept quite simple, with nothing added to the prayer book rite. The more elaborate services are sometimes called "high church"; the simpler ones, "low church." To an extent, these variations reflect the denomination's varied history.

While a good deal of freedom is allowed in local parishes concerning worship as well as theological views, the structure of the Episcopal Church helps to keep all varieties of belief and worship under one roof.

Three Orders of Clergy

Following the Roman Catholic tradition, the Episcopal Church has three orders of clergy. It has bishops, whose connection with the original apostles is maintained through the historic episcopate. Bishops ordain clergy and administer confirmation. Priests, or presbyters, are men and women who work mostly as pastors of parishes. Their primary job is to administer the sacraments, preach, and teach. The third order is the diaconate. Deacons assist priests. Their ordination is sometimes seen as something like a doctor's internship; after a certain length of time, many deacons are ordained as priests. Others remain in what is known as the perpetual diaconate, a ministry devoted to acts of service, particularly to people who are poor, sick, and lonely. In addition, lay readers are people licensed to conduct certain services and to help with the administration of holy communion.

Ecumenical Participation

In recent years the ecumenical movement has been a major concern of Episcopalians. The Episcopal Church has been active in organizations such as the National Council of Churches and the Consultation on Church Union. The General Convention has endorsed church efforts toward ecumenism, though no merger with other denominations is anticipated.

An example of the direction in which such efforts have led is the establishment of full communion between the Episcopal Church and the Evangelical Lutheran Church in America. This agreement, affirming a common understanding of the Christian faith and mutual recognition of baptism and the sharing of the Lord's supper, was ratified by both bodies in 1999. Given their history, Episcopalians are concerned that ecumenical efforts also include Roman Catholics and, like all Anglicans, seek to close the gaps between churches.

Facing World Problems

For many years the church has maintained social agencies, hospitals, and schools in an effort to address human need. Episcopal friars, monks, and nuns, for instance, have done much selfless work with people and parishes experiencing poverty. The General Convention has allocated millions of dollars for work in urban neighborhoods, Latin America, and Africa. Parishes in cities have received much attention, both on the national and the diocesan level. The Presiding Bishop's Fund for World Relief works both alone and ecumenically to deal with both domestic and foreign crises of hunger, refugee resettlement, and development.

Because of its English roots, the Episcopal Church remained for many years a predominantly white Anglo-Saxon church. Over the past century, however, a concerted effort has been made to reach out to the African American, Asian, Native American, and Hispanic communities. A significant number of parishes now bring the Anglican tradition and worship to a non-Anglo constituency. Indeed, today the majority of Anglicans in the world are people of color.

For Discussion

1. How does the Episcopal Church's development as a separate denomination compare with that of the ELCA?

2. What are some similarities and differences between Episcopal teachings and those of your church? Are the differences important? Why or why not?

3. Do you think you would feel comfortable worshiping in an Episcopal church? Why or why not?

For Further Study

· *The Episcopal Handbook* (Morehouse, 2015)
· *Welcome to the Book of Common Prayer* by Vicki K. Black (Morehouse, 2005)
· *Welcome to the Episcopal Church: An Introduction to Its History, Faith, and Worship* by Christopher L. Webber (Morehouse, 1999)
· Episcopal Church website: www.episcopalchurch.org

Table of Comparison

	Episcopalians	*Lutherans*
Teachings	1. Accept Apostles' and Nicene Creeds. 2. Accept the Bible as the word of God. 3. Celebrate two sacraments; observe five additional sacramentals. 4. Believe in Christ's real presence in communion; some explain it as only spiritual; others are close to the Roman Catholic view of transubstantiation. 5. Understand apostolic succession as bishops ordained in an unbroken line back to the apostles.	1. Same. 2. Same. 3. Celebrate two sacraments: baptism and communion. 4. Believe in Christ's real presence in communion, that the communicant receives the body and blood of Christ with the bread and wine. 5. Understand apostolic succession as continuity with the apostles' teaching.
Type of Worship	Liturgical. Form for main service fixed in the *Book of Common Prayer* and subject to change by General Convention.	Liturgical, following the tradition of the Western church.
Governance	An episcopal form with three ranks of clergy: bishops, priests, and deacons. The government of the Episcopal Church is democratic, and congregations have considerable freedom.	Interdependent congregational, regional, national, and global expressions of the church are characterized by democratic decision making, strong ecumenical relationships, elected leadership, and an ordained ministry.
Statistics	Membership: 1,951,907 Congregations: 6,794	

CHAPTER 14

EVANGELICAL COVENANT CHURCH

The Evangelical Covenant Church accepts the Old and New Testaments as the word of God and the only perfect rule for faith, doctrine, and conduct.

Within the relatively formal Swedish Lutheran Church in the nineteenth century, movements sprang up that called for Christians to have a personal experience of grace. These movements, combined with aspects of English Evangelicalism, had significant influence on the life of a young Uppsala University student, Carl Olof Rosenius. This influence would bear fruit as Rosenius became the leader of the evangelical movement in Sweden. Within the evangelical movement, the Mission Covenant of Sweden was born in 1878. This was a "free church" because it was not a part of the Lutheran State Church of Sweden.

Mission Friends

Mission Covenant beliefs were carried to the United States by young immigrants forming faith communities called "Mission Friends." In this country many of them affiliated with the Augustana Lutheran Church, which eventually became part of the Evangelical Lutheran Church in America. But when some of these Mission Friends decided that too many church members were giving little evidence of new life in Christ, they began to seek fellowship elsewhere. In 1885 the Mission Friends organized the Evangelical Covenant Church of America. These people emphasized a good life above doctrine, congregational polity, and a free liturgy, and they insisted on evidence of new life. They had a great interest in evangelism and missions.

Today the Covenant Church is a small but vital denomination. Its active concern for Christian education and nurture, evangelism and outreach, missions, and social responsibility mark it as a church eager to be relevant in today's world. Like many other Christians, they seek to translate their faith into accessible language so it can touch the lives of people from many different ethnic backgrounds.

While the Covenant Church does not belong to either the World Council of Churches or the National Council of Churches, it does cooperate with several of their agencies. Some of its members have served in significant leadership roles.

Conservative in Theology

The Evangelical Covenant Church shares a theologically conservative and evangelical heritage within Protestantism. It accepts the holy scriptures, the Old and the New Testaments, as the word of God and the only perfect rule for faith, doctrine, and conduct. It values the historic confessions of the Christian church, particularly the Apostles' Creed; however, it has not made subscription to a particular creed a requirement for membership in the church.

The Covenant Church follows classical trinitarian beliefs. God's love and mercy are fully revealed in Jesus Christ. Jesus Christ shared our human situation, experienced our anguish, despair, alienation, guilt, and condemnation. Through Christ's death and resurrection, God overcame the power of sin and released us from its bondage. The atonement is for all people, but its benefits are known only to those who participate in faith.

Human beings were created in God's image for fellowship with God. Created as free moral agents, humans have now fallen into sin through their own choice. Original sin holds the human race in a bondage from which it cannot, through its own will, extricate itself. Our sin is essentially our desire to manage our lives on our own terms without calling on God. Salvation becomes a reality only when we confess our sin, admit our inability to save ourselves, and wholeheartedly place our trust in the grace of God. We are justified, not by our works, but solely by faith, which is itself made possible through the grace of God.

The Gathered Church

The Covenant Church holds to the ideal of the *gathered*, or *believers*, church. Only people who have personally accepted Christ as Savior and Lord and live in a way that does not contradict that confession are members of the true church. The denomination does not ask for uniformity in matters that are not central to the faith. Members must, however, hold themselves subject to the authority of scripture.

Baptism and holy communion are divinely ordained sacraments. While the Covenant Church has traditionally practiced the baptism of infants, both those who accept adult baptism and those who accept infant baptism belong to the fellowship. It requires that its ministers recognize the validity of infant as well as adult baptism and administer either form when so requested.

Worship is dignified, but without elaborate liturgy. Faithful preaching of the word is emphasized in the conviction that the entire life of God's people must be shaped by the living Word. Music also plays a large role in Covenant worship.

The doctrine of the priesthood of all believers is central. Christ's ministry is carried on through the church as a whole, and every member has a responsibility to witness to the gospel. This ministry includes concern for physical and social as well as spiritual needs of people. The purpose of both the social and spiritual concern is to bring others to acceptance of Christ and to glorify God through realizing God's will in the world.

For Discussion

1. What signs do you see that the Covenant Church's origins lie within the Lutheran church?

2. What points of difference do you see between the two?

3. How important do you think it is that each church member lives in a way that gives evidence of his or her faith?

For Further Study

· *Anatomy of the Pilgrim Experience: Reflections on Being a Covenanter* by Zenos Hawkinson (Covenant, 2000)

· *By One Spirit* by Karl A. Olsson (Covenant, 2002)

· *Covenant Affirmations: This We Believe* by Donald C. Frisk and Milton B. Engebretson (Covenant, 1981)

· Evangelical Covenant Church website: www.covchurch.org

Table of Comparison

	Evangelical Covenant	*Lutherans*
Teachings	1. Accept the Bible as the word of God.	1. Accept the Bible as the written witness to God's revelation through Jesus Christ.
	2. Believe in the triune nature of God.	2. Same.
	3. Believe in the full divinity and humanity of Christ.	3. Same.
	4. Teach justification by grace through faith.	4. Same.
	5. Practice a gathered church.	5. See the church as called by the gospel through word and sacrament.
	6. Accept baptism and holy communion as sacraments. Either adult or infant baptism may be practiced, but the infant form is traditional.	6. Celebrate sacraments of baptism and holy communion. Unbaptized adults are baptized, but infant baptism is regular practice.
Type of Worship	Dignified but without elaborate liturgy. Emphasis on preaching of the word.	Liturgical patterns utilized with emphasis on preaching of the word and celebration of the sacraments.
Governance	Member congregations support policies and programs of the Covenant Church while maintaining broad freedom in local matters.	Interdependent congregational, regional, national, and global expressions of the church are characterized by democratic decision making, strong ecumenical relationships, elected leadership, and an ordained ministry.
Statistics	Membership: 228,365 Congregations: 816	

CHAPTER 15

EVANGELICAL FREE CHURCH

Worship in the Evangelical Free Church is orderly without being extremely formal.

Freedom has been a question of considerable importance for many people in the history of the Christian church. Some people have wanted freedom to interpret the Bible as they pleased. Others have sought freedom from ecclesiastical or civil authority. Such a concern for freedom was evident among many immigrants. For some people, it was the main motivation for coming to America. Not surprisingly, many of these immigrants established churches that were free from all organizational ties. In this way, they hoped to have the freedom they sought.

Free Churches

Scandinavian immigrants were already acquainted with a "free church" concept. For a number of years, groups of people had held meetings separate from the state churches. Once on American soil, these immigrants continued these free meetings with only a minimum amount of organization.

During the early part of the twentieth century, there were enough free congregations that two national organizations were formed for fellowship. The Swedish Evangelical Free Church of the United States of America was incorporated in 1908, and the Norwegian-Danish Evangelical Free Church Association of North America was formed in 1912. These two organizations merged in 1950 to form the Evangelical Free Church of America.

Worship and Practice

The Evangelical Free Church takes a strong stand on the authority of the Bible. It believes that the scriptures, including both the Old and New Testaments, are the inspired word of God, without error in the original writings.

In all doctrine and church organization, the denomination seeks to follow its best interpretations of the scriptures. These beliefs are summarized in a twelve-article statement that was adopted at the time of the merger. Major points in that statement of faith include an affirmation of the triune nature of God as Father, Son, and Holy Spirit. Also confessed is the fallen, sinful condition of humanity. In this lost condition, eternal life is obtained only through regeneration by the Holy Spirit. Although salvation is made possible by the death of Christ, it must be claimed by each individual through a personal belief in Jesus and acceptance of him as Savior. Qualification for church membership is based on evidence of conversion and living the Christian life.

Two ordinances are practiced: the Lord's supper and baptism. The Free Church follows the tradition of Zwingli rather than Luther concerning the Lord's supper. It believes that Christ is present in the communion service only in a spiritual sense, and not in a real way. Baptism is considered to be a demonstration to the world that salvation has taken place. It is not seen as a means of salvation. Both immersion and sprinkling are permitted within the framework of the statement of faith. At present, more congregations practice immersion than sprinkling.

There is no single pattern of worship in congregations. Services generally include singing hymns, reading scripture, and listening to a sermon preached by the congregation's minister. These services are orderly without being extremely formal, although the amount of formality varies from church to church.

Organization for Fellowship

The congregations have a congregational form of government and are united for fellowship and cooperative work in the Evangelical Free Church of America. According to the articles of incorporation, this structure enables "such mutual activities beyond the scope and ability of a congregation." At the same time, it is declared that the Evangelical Free Church organization has "no controlling power over the internal affairs" of the congregations. The congregation calls its own pastor, who has been prepared through training and ordination to minister to the spiritual needs of the people.

Social Attitudes

Although the denomination believes that Christians should be concerned about the problems that face society, direct social action has never been a major thrust. It does have a Committee on Social Concern that makes recommendations to the general conference concerning involvement in social problems. Much of the denomination's ministry of social action is done through cooperative effort with several other denominations in the National Association of Evangelicals.

For Discussion

1. Why do you think a "free church" might have been attractive to immigrants?
2. How does an Evangelical Free Church congregation's complete freedom compare with the way your congregation is organized?
3. How might the idea that the Bible is without error in the original writings interfere with one's relationship with God? How might it be helpful?

For Further Study

· *Evangelical Convictions*, ed. Greg Strand and Bill Kynes (Free Church, 2011)
· Evangelical Free Church of America website: www.efca.org

Table of Comparison

	Evangelical Free	Lutherans
Teachings	1. Believe the Bible is the word of God.	1. Believe the Bible is the written witness to God's revelation of saving action through Jesus Christ.
	2. Believe in the triune nature of God.	2. Same.
	3. Believe in the full divinity and full humanity of Christ.	3. Same.
	4. Teach justification by faith.	4. Teach justification by grace through faith.
	5. Consider baptism and holy communion as symbols.	5. Celebrate sacraments of baptism and holy communion as means of God's grace.
	6. Affirm the presence of Christ in holy communion only in a spiritual sense.	6. Affirm the real presence of Christ in holy communion.
Type of Worship	Somewhat informal with no stated liturgy.	Liturgical, following primary pattern of the Western church.
Governance	Congregational form with each local church in complete control of its own affairs.	Interdependent congregational, regional, national, and global expressions of the church are characterized by democratic decision making, strong ecumenical relationships, elected leadership, and an ordained ministry.
Statistics	Membership: 357,186 Congregations: 1,470	

CHAPTER 16

EVANGELICAL LUTHERAN CHURCH IN AMERICA

Martin Luther nailed his Ninety-Five Theses *on the door of the Wittenberg Castle Church on October 31, 1517.*

For many who are using this book, *Lutheran* would describe not "our neighbor's faith" but our own. Still, in the context of all these churches and denominations, examining again how the Lutheran church came to be what it is and what we believe is helpful.

The Reformation of the sixteenth century divided the church in Europe. Yet this division was not Martin Luther's original purpose; he wanted only to reform and renew the existing church. He did not want to begin a separate denomination of Christians, much less a church that bears his name. Luther's sole concern was proper biblical teaching for the "one, holy, catholic, and apostolic" church. Unfortunately, this concern led Luther and other reformers into conflict with the teachings of the Roman church of the time. The resulting body, the Lutheran church, is both protestant and catholic.

Radical Focus on Grace

If you were to boil down Lutheran beliefs to one word, a strong candidate for that word would be *grace*. Lutherans teach that we are who we are because of God's grace—that is, God's love for us without our deserving it in any way. This grace is shown in countless ways, but most clearly in the good news that we are saved only through the death and resurrection of Jesus Christ. That is the gospel, the kernel of our life and hope, and all else is secondary to this.

Most, if not all, Christian churches also point to God's grace, but Lutherans tend to give it greater emphasis. They say that anything added to the gospel of Jesus Christ, whether as a source of life or requirement for living, is misguided. It may be well meaning, even beneficial, but it must not be put on the same level as the gospel.

So, for instance, other traditional teachings can be helpful, but if they don't have biblical support, Lutherans would say we cannot be bound to them. Lutheran worship is usually built on the classical Western church pattern, but that is not required. Christians are not required to be "born again" or to live in a certain way as evidence of their faith—and perhaps only then be baptized. In that case, a lifestyle has been added to the gospel. Of course, Christians will want to live good, moral lives, but we are not saved by what we do, only by God's free grace given to sinners and even infants.

Justification by Grace through Faith

While Lutherans agree with all Christians that faith involves personal commitment and should result in our living our lives for others, they shy away from using outward signs of commitment or service to decide whether a person really has faith. After all, we all fail at times to do the right thing. These failures, according to Lutheran teaching, reveal what kind of people we really are by stripping away illusions and pride. We learn about our weakness and vulnerability, and the depth of sin. We begin to learn how much we need the mercy and understanding of others. At such times we may be particularly open to the message of the gospel, because the gospel tells us that God accepts people despite our failures.

Lutherans see the fact that God accepts us in spite of our sinfulness as the heart of the teaching of Jesus. We see it in Bible passages such as the parable of the prodigal son. The gospel teaches that God forgives us even though we have failed. Because Jesus died on the cross for us, God receives us. We can turn to God in our troubled times. We have a place to go, and God rejoices in our homecoming.

No one—no matter how good—can ever earn his or her own salvation. The law, God's demands, convinces us that we need the gospel. Our only source of hope is the gospel's assurance of God's grace freely given to the ungodly through Jesus Christ. This teaching Lutherans call "justification by grace through faith alone."

The Word of God

Lutherans hold a number of teachings in common with the vast majority of other Christian denominations. One of the most important teachings concerns the understanding of the word of God. Lutherans commonly speak of the word of God in three senses.

First, the word of God is Jesus Christ himself, who was "in the beginning . . . with God" and indeed "was God" (John 1:1). This same Word "became flesh and lived among us" (John 1:14).

Second, the word of God is the message about Jesus Christ—his life, death, and resurrection. This is the subject of the New Testament and the subject to which the Old Testament points as it tells of God's work of salvation among the people of Israel. In this sense, the "word of God" means the same as the "gospel"—the good news of Jesus Christ that is proclaimed by believers (see 1 Peter 1:24-25). This sense of the word of God protects Lutherans from the danger of worshiping the Bible. God's word is good news that cannot be imprisoned in type. It must be proclaimed in every generation with a living voice.

Third, Lutherans affirm that the word of God is the whole Bible, Old and New Testaments. The Bible helps to ensure that the church remains faithful to the gospel. It protects the people of God from false teaching and tells them the rich and varied story of God's work of salvation. The Bible is the record of divine revelation and the final authority for all preaching and teaching. No doctrine or tradition of the church overrules it or adds to it. The Reformation had an appropriate slogan: *sola scriptura*—scripture alone!

The Means of Grace

Lutherans celebrate the sacraments of baptism and the Lord's supper. (Some Lutherans, based on the Lutheran Confessions, also consider confession and absolution to be a sacrament.) Sacraments are specific, external signs instituted by Christ himself that convey God's grace and mercy. The sacraments use the common elements of water, bread, and wine transformed by the word of God into means of salvation.

Baptism is the entryway into the church. Following ancient Christian practice, Lutherans baptize infants, an action that is in line with their belief that we are saved by God's grace, not by anything we could possibly do. Baptism begins the journey of faith, yet it is to be acknowledged daily in the Christian life.

Christ also instituted the Lord's supper "on the night when he was betrayed" (1 Corinthians 11:23). The Lord's supper is the true body and blood of Christ sacrificed for us beginning on that night long ago. It nourishes the believer throughout life, assuring the believer of forgiveness from sin and of the presence of God in what is often a dark and hostile world.

Preaching the gospel and sharing the sacraments are, according to Lutheran teaching, the work of the church. Where these are performed, there the church is to be found. This definition of the church is truly ecumenical. The church does not need a certain sign on the door. It does not need a specific form of church government. The church is the word of God, the sacraments of baptism and the Lord's supper, and sinners seeking God's grace. Where these are found, there the church lives. That is also why coming together in worship is so important for Lutherans. That is where we hear the word preached and receive the sacraments.

Christian Service: Faith Active in Love

Finally, Lutherans know with all Christians that true faith is actively expressed in love for our neighbor. As Jesus sought the outcast and outsider in his ministry, so the church seeks them in its ministry. The church is called to serve people's material as well as spiritual needs. All Christians are called to such service: "Truly I tell you, just as you did it to one of the least of these who are members of my family, you did it to me" (Matthew 25:40).

The Lutheran Landscape

Most of what has been said regarding Lutheran beliefs applies to all Lutherans; however, as is true of many families of churches, Lutherans are divided. Some of these divisions are for ethnic reasons: people from different areas (primarily in Western Europe) had different languages and varying national allegiances that carried over for some of them as they immigrated to America. Other divisions have to do with disagreements over doctrine and church practice. Splits have occurred over matters as diverse as whether it is proper to take out insurance, how much authority denominational leaders should have, and whether women should be ordained into the ministry.

The two largest Lutheran denominations in the United States are the Evangelical Lutheran Church in America (ELCA) and the Lutheran Church—Missouri Synod (LCMS). The ELCA is the larger of the two and the publisher of this book. The LCMS is considered in its own chapter on page 82. Besides these two, the Wisconsin Evangelical Lutheran Synod (WELS) has about 400,000 members, and a number of other small Lutheran groups exist in the United States.

As this book demonstrates, many divisions within Christianity have occurred, but the ELCA is the result of a long line of mergers. Most of the Lutheran bodies that eventually formed the ELCA came from German, Norwegian, and Swedish roots, though other nationalities are also represented. The ELCA was formed in 1987 through the merger of three Lutheran denominations, the American Lutheran Church (itself a product of four groups with Norwegian, German, and Danish roots), the Lutheran Church in America (which included people with Swedish, German, Danish, Finnish, and Slovak roots), and the small Association of Evangelical Lutheran Churches (congregations that separated from the LCMS in the 1970s).

The Evangelical Lutheran Church in America tends toward the middle in the spectrum of American Christianity regarding both doctrine and social issues. It looks to the Bible for authority in its preaching and teaching yet does not take a literalist approach to scripture. It wrestles with thorny social issues, but its positions are neither wildly liberal nor rigidly conservative. With most mainline Protestant churches, it supports the ordination of women to the ministry.

Ecumenically, it has been an enthusiastic partner in dialogues with other denominations, and, where possible without compromising its beliefs, it has entered into fellowship with them. Growing from deep, strong roots, it is intent on reaching out with the good news of Jesus Christ.

For Discussion

1. What would you consider the greatest strengths of the ELCA? The greatest weaknesses?

2. If you are a member of an ELCA congregation that is older than the ELCA (that is, begun before 1987), what are its historical roots?

3. Why do you belong to the denomination you are a member of?

For Further Study

· *The Book of Concord: The Confessions of the Evangelical Lutheran Church*, ed. Robert Kolb and Timothy J. Wengert (Fortress, 2000)

· *The Lutheran Handbook: A Field Guide to Church Stuff, Everyday Stuff, and the Bible* by Kristofer Skrade (Augsburg Fortress, 2005)

· *Lutheran Questions, Lutheran Answers* by Martin E. Marty (Augsburg Fortress, 2007)

· Evangelical Lutheran Church in America website: www.elca.org

ELCA Full Communion Partners

Presbyterian Church (U.S.A.), since 1997
Reformed Church in America, since 1997
United Church of Christ, since 1997
Episcopal Church, since 1999
Moravian Church, since 1999
United Methodist Church, since 2009

Statistics   Membership: 4,181,219
                      Congregations: 9,846

CHAPTER 17

HINDUISM (VEDANTA)

A worshiper lights incense before the image of a Hindu deity.

The religion known to most Westerners as Hinduism encompasses many different spiritual traditions and practices. These religious sects are unified by their reliance on ancient texts called the Vedas as the primary source of inspiration and the basis for philosophy and spiritual practice. The Vedas are considered to be timeless truths revealed to anonymous sages at least four to five thousand years ago. *Veda* means "knowledge" in Sanskrit.

The primary philosophy based on the Vedas is called Vedanta, literally meaning "the culmination of the Vedas." There are four Vedas, each with four parts. The last and most philosophical portion of each Veda contains the Upanishads, climactic texts on which the Vedantic philosophy of Hinduism is based.

The three main schools of Vedantic philosophy are categorized according to whether God (Brahman) and creation are understood as separate (dualism); creation is the parts, God is the whole (qualified nondualism); or God and creation are united (nondualism or *Advaita*). Each of these schools attempts to address the universal and timeless mystery: the relationship between God, humankind, and nature. The easiest way to explain the various schools of thought as well as the practice of different sects is to start with Advaita Vedanta as taught by Shankaracharya, a seventh-century philosopher-saint.

The Nature of Brahman and the Universe

Use of the term *Brahman* is common to all schools of Vedanta. It is used in much the same way "God" is used in other religious traditions—to refer to the highest, most exalted entity, the Absolute. According to Vedantic philosophy, the goal of life is to establish an ultimate union with this ultimate reality.

In Hindu thought, this universe is an illusion of that one reality. All that we see and experience merely appears to be real. The power of Brahman to project this apparent reality is known as *maya*. Ignorance causes us to perceive what we see and experience as real.

The Nature of Human Beings

Our true nature is divine, emerging from Brahman. We fail to realize our own divine nature because we believe what our senses tell us. They take in what seems to be a finite, divided, changing universe that follows laws of causation, and we assume that is reality. Our genetic programming, as well as our scientific worldview, make us identify with our body and mind. We feel finite, separated from the rest of the universe, and subject to change, disease, and death.

The goal of life, as understood by Hinduism, is to see through our mistake and realize our true nature. As seen within the illusion of space and time, we are individual souls, *jivas*, seeking to be reunited with that absolute Brahman, called the *Paramatman*.

Karma and Reincarnation

Within this world of time, space, and causation, things appear to work in certain ways. The laws of physics tell us that for every action there is a reaction. Every one of our actions, thoughts, and desires creates a kind of vibrational impression (*samskara*) on us. The law of karma states that until one transcends this relative plane of existence and is reunited with Brahman, every action will have its reaction. Our karma (actions) may not bear fruit in this life but may be stored until a future life. At the time of death, if an individual has not yet realized his or her divine nature, the soul (*jiva*) after death may experience heavenly or hellish realms until he or she reincarnates in a new body. The options available to the jiva are restricted according to the stored karmas and the lessons that need to be learned.

Ways of Thinking about This World

Because the world is a misperception of reality, there is uncertainty about it. This apparent universe of ours can be thought of as the dream of Brahman, who has projected this universe and entered into it, just as we enter a dream world when we sleep. Our dream world often has little reality compared to our waking state. We project the dream and enter into it. Similarly, our perception of this world has no reality when compared to the realization of God.

Why do we misperceive Brahman (God) to be this world of duality? From within maya (the illusory world), there is no answer. Beyond maya (in the true existence with Brahman), the question does not arise. The closest we can understand is to say that God "creates" the world as a divine play (*lila*).

Duality, Gods, and Goddesses

When the One appears manifest as many, it must do so in pairs of opposites. Dividing everything using names and forms is also a major characteristic of this cosmic dream.

We can think of Brahman as being like a stringed instrument. Music is like the creation. The vibrations of the sound occur equally in both directions, as pairs of opposites. The various levels of existence from the gross world to such subtle levels as our mental plane, or heavenly planes of existence, are like octaves of each other.

The male-female duality is sometimes used to symbolize and personify the active and inactive aspects of the absolute Brahman. The active principle is the feminine: the Divine Mother. Hinduism also uses three god/goddess pairs to personify the three aspects of the manifest world: creation, preservation, and destruction. Other sects see all three aspects in one deity. It is important to remember that all the various gods and goddesses of Hinduism are but aspects of Brahman (the absolute one God) as seen through maya.

Waking Up through Spiritual Practices

Because our true nature is infinite, undivided, and unchanging, we naturally seek to find those qualities within this world. Our yearning for freedom, love, and peace in this world can be seen as our attempt at discovering, respectively, our true infinite, undivided, and unchanging nature. But in the world, the more we get of one, the less we have of one of the other two. Only through spiritual practices can one "wake up" to his or her true nature and find absolute freedom, love, and peace. Hinduism recognizes that all the various religious paths can lead one to God. All the seeming contradictions disappear when the goal is realized. Only pure peace, pure love, and pure freedom remain.

We can help ourselves to wake up to our true nature in many ways. Here is some general advice.

· Remember that your true nature is divine and that, after a series of life cycles through reincarnation, you will reach the goal.

· Accept yourself where you are, and go forward from there.

· Choose the path that best fits your temperament and your natural inclinations. Give your activities a spiritual turn. Figure out ways you can best remember God.

· The goal is to realize or attain your oneness with God. The two main obstacles are forgetting that the world is God in disguise and thus being distracted by your senses, and letting your ego think you are separate and different from others.

Hinduism recognizes specific forms of spiritual practices (yogas) for realizing our true nature. Four of these yogas are:

· *Karma Yoga*—pursuing the path of selfless action. Do your work with the attitude of unselfishness and detachment from the results. Do not expect to make the world perfect. See and serve the divine in other beings.

· *Jnana Yoga*—affirming your true nature. Say, "I am not the mind. I am not the body. I am pure existence, pure consciousness, pure bliss."

· *Bhakti Yoga*—developing a loving relationship with a personal aspect of God. Choose a deity (god or goddess) or an incarnation of God. Relate everything in your life to the chosen deity. Perform a ceremony (sacrament) called a *puja* or worship. The puja gives the worshiper the aid of physical objects and actions to keep the worshiper's mind on the chosen form of God.

· *Raja Yoga*—gaining control over the mind. This is done through meditation, calming the mind to get a clear view of its true nature. Repetition of sacred words or mantras and breath control help to amplify the spiritual vibrations.

Classifying Various Hindu Beliefs

As noted above, the two other main schools of Vedantic philosophy are qualified nondualism (rather than thinking you are one with God, you think you are a part of God like a spark from the fire) and dualism (you and God are separate, and the goal is to be eternally in God's presence).

Sometimes Hinduism is divided into groups according to which deity is the primary focus of worship. All deities are accepted as manifestations of the one Brahman, but different groups view different deities as the highest manifestation or the most efficacious to worship. Each is like a different doorway to reach the one Brahman.

Tantra is another Advaitic (nondual) philosophy. Whereas Shankara's Advaita Vedanta emphasizes the unreality of the world compared with Brahman, Tantra emphasizes that this world is nothing but Shakti, the power of Brahman—Brahman in disguise to be worshiped as the Divine Mother. Our consciousness should be trained to see Shakti or the Divine Mother in everything, to use everything as a reminder of the all-pervading oneness. All the yogas can still be followed with slight changes in attitude.

Organizations and Hinduism

Hinduism is not centrally organized. It did not start with one person or group from which others broke away. Many temples are independent entities where people come to worship. Traditionally, study of the scriptures was done by independent teachers (gurus) who had experienced God in a transcendental way, some of whom would give initiation into certain spiritual practices. It was primarily one group of Hindus, the Brahmin caste of India, who were responsible for learning the scriptures. Most homes would have a family shrine where their chosen deity would be worshiped every day.

Today, in addition to independent temples, there are organizations with centers throughout India and the world, the Ramakrishna Order being one of the largest. It is inspired by Sri Ramakrishna (1836–1886), who lived in Bengal, India. He followed all paths described above as well as Christian and Islamic traditions and realized the same oneness with God through each, proving that the same goal can be reached by various paths. There are now fifteen centers in the United States headed by swamis of the Ramakrishna Order founded by Swami Vivekananda (1863–1902), a disciple of Sri Ramakrishna. Today there are many groups representing all sects and traditions of Hinduism. As more Indians come to live in this country, individual Hindu temples are being built.

Because Hinduism accepts all traditions as valid approaches to God, most Hindu groups have no missionary zeal, no need to convert others. But because of its all-encompassing nature, Vedantic philosophy is adaptable to any culture and country and is being studied and accepted by many Westerners. The influence of Vedantic ideas can be seen in groups not classified as Hindu. Hindus believe that by studying different religions, they can come to a deeper understanding of their own.

For Discussion

1. Have you had any exposure to Hindu people or beliefs? If so, how have these influenced your opinion of Hinduism?

2. Compare the Hindu understanding of Brahman as the only reality with the Christian belief in a separate, sovereign God. How might this difference affect how you look at life?

3. Look at the descriptions of the four yogas. Could some of these be useful for Christians? Could some of them work against Christian beliefs? How or why?

For Further Study

· *The Bhagavad-Gita: Classic of Indian Spirituality*, 2nd. ed., trans. Eknath Easwaran (Nilgiri, 2007)

· *The Essentials of Hinduism: A Comprehensive Overview of the World's Oldest Religion*, 2nd ed., by Swami Bhaskarananda (Viveka, 2002)

· *Many Gods of Hinduism* by Swami Achuthananda (CreateSpace Independent Publishing Platform, 2013)

· *The Upanishads*, 2nd ed., trans. Eknath Easwaran (Nilgiri, 2007)

· Websites:
  - Vedanta Society of Southern California: vedanta.org
  - Ramakrishna Vedanta Society: vedantasociety.net
  - Advaita Vedanta Home Page: www.advaita-vedanta.org

Table of Comparison

	Advaita Vedanta	Lutherans
Teachings	1. Understand Brahman as the Absolute; however, Brahman is seen as various manifestations, such as Rama/Sita and Krishna/Radha. 2. Believe the universe is an illusion, a misperception of the one reality that is Brahman. 3. Believe our goal in life is to realize that we are one with Brahman. 4. Believe in karma, the law of cause and effect. 5. Teach that the path to realizing our oneness with Brahman may take many lifetimes, in which we may take many forms.	1. Believe in a personal, triune God— Father, Son, Holy Spirit. These persons remain unchanged through eternity. 2. Believe all things are created by God and are subject to God. God is separate from creation, which includes humans. 3. Teach that we are alienated from God, but through Christ's death, we are saved and brought back to God. 4. Believe that although humans have the freedom to disobey God, all is under the umbrella of God's law and grace. 5. Teach that we are created as unique humans, and we each have one earthly life.
Type of Worship	Meditation, repetition of mantras or holy words. Remembering and honoring Brahman with offerings of flowers, food, and incense.	Liturgical, following the tradition of the Western church.
Governance	No overall government. Generally, spiritual direction is provided by the head of the local center, often with an elected board of directors.	Interdependent congregational, regional, national, and global expressions of the church are characterized by democratic decision making, strong ecumenical relationships, elected leadership, and an ordained ministry.
Statistics	Membership: 641,186 Congregations: 1,625	

CHAPTER 18

ISLAM

*Prayer (salah) is a pillar of the Islam faith
and is performed at least five times a day.*

More than one-fifth of the world's population follows Islam, and only Christianity is believed to have more adherents. The Muslim objective is to live for the pleasure of Allah, who created humankind to serve him only in order to reach the ultimate goal of paradise in the next life. (*Allah* means "the One, the Only" and is one of the many names of God.)

Islam is the name of the religion; the term means "peace" or "submission" in Arabic. One who practices Islam is *Muslim.* (Moslem is an older, less correct spelling.) Muslims were among the earliest settlers in North America. Certain customs of slaves in the 1700s can be traced to their Islamic heritage. Arabs who came to the United States in the early 1900s practiced Islam in their homes, and so Islam was not highly visible in the general community. More recently, however, news media brought Islam notoriety through coverage of Nobel Drew Ali (Marcus Garvey or Elijah Muhammad), Malcolm X, the Gulf War, the 2001 attack on the World Trade Towers in New York City, ongoing conflict throughout the Middle East and elsewhere, and many other people and events.

More than forty countries around the world have Muslim populations. Indonesia has the largest concentration, followed by Pakistan, India, and Bangladesh. In the United States, Islam is commonly considered the fastest-growing religion. The U.S. has six to eight million Muslims, including immigrants, recent converts, and first- and second-generation Muslim Americans.

Source of Muslim Beliefs

Islam is based on the teachings of Muhammad ibn Abdullah, who lived around 570–632. When Muhammad was forty years old, he received his first revelation from Allah. Whenever he received a revelation, he recited it to his followers, who memorized and wrote down every word. Over a period of twenty-three years, Allah's revelations through the archangel Gabriel to the prophet Muhammad were collected and became the holy Qur'an (sometimes spelled Koran). The collected revelation appeals to reason and serves as a guide and warning to all humankind. What is lawful and unlawful, the resulting rewards and punishments, and the criteria for justice are clearly outlined in it.

Muslims implement to the best of their ability the lifestyle contained in the Qur'an and the traditions and sayings of the prophet Muhammad. They hold to the Pillars of Islam, the foundation and strength of their faith:

· Faith (*iman*)—reciting the central creed of Islam, testifying to Allah's oneness: "There is none worthy of worship except God, and Muhammad is the messenger of God."

· Prayer (*salah*)—performing ritual prayers at least five times a day.

· Charity (*zakah*)—after taking care of the necessities of life, giving an annual donation of 2.5 percent of wealth to people who are poor.

· Fasting (*sawm*)—abstaining from food and drink (children and people who are sick are exempt) between sunrise and sunset during Ramadan, the ninth month of the lunar calendar.

· Pilgrimage (*hajj*)—traveling to Mecca, Saudi Arabia, to perform ordained rituals seeking Allah's forgiveness and mercy. Every physically, mentally, and financially able Muslim is to undertake this journey once in a lifetime.

Muslims do not consider Islam to be a religion separate from the rest of life. Rather, Islam is for them a complete system of life, encompassing all of existence, including physical, mental, social, spiritual, and academic aspects. In addition, although congregational prayer service (or *jumuah*) is conducted every Friday at every *masjid*, or mosque, no special day of worship or sabbath is recognized in Islam. The Muslim prays five obligatory prayers daily, as well as numerous voluntary prayers, and remains in constant remembrance of Allah by reciting his praises. Thus the Muslim makes every day a day of worship.

Beliefs of Muslims

Islam is found in many different cultures, and sometimes what we think is a characteristic of Islam is actually related to a particular culture, such as the Arabic culture. The Principles of Faith, however, constitute shared common knowledge among Muslims and result in the universal oneness of the worldwide Islamic community.

The cornerstone of Islam is that Allah is one. This monotheism is the foundation of its creed. Beyond that the Principles of Faith, which direct the heart and behavior, include beliefs in the following:

· Allah
· his angels
· his books
· his messengers
· the day of judgment
· life after death
· divine preordainment

Muslims believe that our life on earth is a temporary trial or test and that eternal life after death is inevitable. Those whose good conduct outweighed the bad in earthly life will enjoy paradise. Those whose bad conduct outweighed the good will suffer the wrath of hell.

Significant differences arise when comparing Muslim and Christian beliefs regarding Jesus. Islam teaches that Jesus was

· created;
· Messiah of Israel;
· a prophet, not God;
· neither crucified nor resurrected;
· one who will return in the last days.

Like Judaism and Christianity, Islam teaches that God created humankind, beginning with Adam and Eve. At their creation, all human beings had imprinted on their essence the creed of Allah's oneship and lordship. Islam varies from Christianity, however, in its teaching that humankind is born without sin and with the capacity to be and do good for the pleasure of Allah and the benefit of the person's own soul. All people have an equal opportunity to choose, by their words and deeds, eternal life in hell or in paradise.

Brief History of Islam

The early years of Islam brought suffering, oppression, abuse, and death for the Muslims. To escape persecution, many sought and received refuge and protection from the Christian king of Ethiopia. Eventually they migrated to Medina, in present-day Saudi Arabia, where they were warmly received. Islam spread within Arabia and beyond its borders. While centralized in the Near East, it moved into central Asia and across northern Africa, eventually crossing the Straits of Gibraltar into Spain.

During the European Dark Ages, Islamic scholars and religious leaders continued to educate themselves through research and study. They excelled in the fields of architecture, education, medicine, economics, science, literature, and the arts. Muslims built libraries, schools and universities, and mosques and developed exceptional communities. European scholars began to study Islam during the Renaissance, resulting in the intermingling of the European and Islamic cultures.

Islam contributed greatly to the restoration of society following World War I. Notable works are still used today in mathematics, physics, chemistry, medicine, astronomy, the works of Aristotle, and much more.

Islamic Community and Customs

Marriage is an important institution within Islam; in fact, it is said that "marriage is half of religion." Muslims believe the foundation of civilized society begins with the family. Marriage, which is ordained by Allah, dignifies society and preserves proper human relations.

Muslim men and women are commanded to dress modestly in garments that do not reveal their physical attributes. The woman covers her hair because it is the crown of her beauty. Covering it dignifies her, her husband, and her family and decreases the attention of men. There is no mandate in the Qur'an or in the life of the prophet to cover the face. However, this is practiced in some cultures.

Rules of conduct teach that a Muslim should not do any of the following:
· worship or share in worship of any deity except Allah
· murder, attack another, or be an aggressor
· break contracts
· commit adultery or fornication
· become intoxicated through use of alcohol, wine, or drugs
· gamble or obtain money through illegal means
· lie, steal, or covet
· commit sodomy or be homosexual
· eat pork or food made with or cooked in pork, unless forced by necessity
· cause fear or discomfort to their neighbor
· be immodest, indecent, vulgar, or decadent
· spy on, be suspicious of, backbite, slander, or gossip about others
· practice discrimination

Islam recognizes two holidays, observed at varying dates each year according to the lunar calendar. Each celebration begins with congregational prayer, followed by a sermon, and includes hearty feasts, gift giving, visiting with family and friends, community festivities, carnivals, and the like. The holidays are *Eidul Fitr*, which celebrates the victory (end) of the obligatory fast of Ramadan, and *Eidul Adha*, which marks the end of the pilgrimage and also recognizes prophet Abraham's devotion and obedience to Allah's command to sacrifice his son. Animals are slaughtered, or sacrificed, and the meat distributed to people who are poor.

Muslims use two terms that are important to their faith practice. The first, often misused and misunderstood, is *jihad*, the challenge to achieve piety, submission, and obedience to Allah. The interpretation as "holy war" is misleading. The second term is *imam*, the respected title given to the leader of an Islamic community or to any devout and respected Muslim who leads the prayers.

What the Prophet Said

The prophet Muhammad taught about a wide variety of practical concerns, including the following:

· racism: "All mankind is from Adam and Eve, an Arab has no superiority over a non-Arab; a white has no superiority over a black nor black over white except by piety."

· monetary interest: "Allah has forbidden you to take interest. . . . You will neither inflict nor suffer inequity. Allah has judged that there shall be no interest."

· religion: "No Prophet or Apostle will come after me and no new faith will be born."

· Satan: "Beware of Satan for the safety of your religion. He has lost all hope of leading you astray in big things, so beware of following him in small things."

· women: "You have certain rights regarding women, but they also have rights over you. Remember that you have taken them as your wives only under Allah's trust and with his permission. . . . Do treat your women well and be kind to them for they are your partners and committed helpers."

For Discussion

1. Muslims will sometimes refer to believers from three religions—Judaism, Christianity, and Islam—as "people of the Book." Why is that an appropriate title?

2. Islam developed after Christianity. Generally, what is our attitude toward later revelations such as this? What are our criteria for determining what religion is true?

3. In what areas do you think Islam is most misunderstood by the average American?

For Further Study

· *In the Footsteps of the Prophet: Lessons from the Life of Muhammad* by Tariq Ramadan (Oxford University Press, 2009)

· *Islam: A Short History* by Karen Armstrong (Modern Library, 2002)

· *No God but God: The Origins, Evolution, and Future of Islam* by Reza Aslan (Random House, 2011)

Table of Comparison

	Muslims	Lutherans
Teachings	1. Believe that God (Allah) is one.	1. Believe in the triune God—one God in three persons.
	2. Believe that revelations to a number of God's prophets, including Jesus, culminated in those to the prophet Muhammad.	2. Believe that Jesus is the Son of God, that his life, death, and resurrection completed God's work of our salvation.
	3. See Islam as a total way of life.	3. See people as instruments of God in the world, not separate from it.
	4. Look to the Qur'an (the words of God through Gabriel to Muhammad) as the primary source for faith and practice.	4. Look to the Bible—Old and New Testaments—as the only written word of God.
	5. Try to live according to the five Pillars of Faith.	5. Have no comparable framework, but look to teachings such as the Ten Commandments and the Sermon on the Mount.
Type of Worship	Congregational prayer held on Friday, during which men and women assemble separately for prayer and hear a sermon by the imam.	Liturgical form typically includes hymns, prayers, readings, sermon, and holy communion based on ecumenical patterns.
Governance	Local Islamic communities led by imams. Explicit rules in Qur'an guide community life.	Interdependent congregational, regional, national, and global expressions of the church are characterized by democratic decision making, strong ecumenical relationships, elected leadership, and an ordained ministry.
Statistics*	Membership: 2,600,000 Congregations: 2,106	

*From *The American Mosque 2011: Basic Characteristics of the American Mosque, Attitudes of Mosque Leaders—Report Number 1 from the US Mosque Study 2011* by Ihsan Bagby (Council on American-Islamic Relations, 2011)

CHAPTER 19

JEHOVAH'S WITNESSES

Witnesses believe that accurate knowledge about God is essential. For this reason they print and distribute Bibles and Bible literature internationally.

Fervently zealous in their convictions, Jehovah's Witnesses accept the entire Bible as the word of God and base their beliefs solely on it, excluding church traditions. They believe they are the only Christians who have such a view of the Bible. They have no clergy, and every one of Jehovah's Witnesses is considered a minister with responsibility to spread the good news of God's kingdom.

Witnesses use the word *church* to refer to a united body of worshipers and not to a building. Ministers of the society see their chief work as bearing witness to the truth on behalf of God, whose name is Jehovah, the source of their name, Jehovah's Witnesses.

Baptism: Symbol Dedication

To become a minister for Jehovah, an individual is instructed to study the Bible to learn God's will, to live in harmony with it, and to make a personal commitment to God, doing so in private prayer to God. As a symbol of this dedication, a person is baptized by immersion in water and thus becomes an ordained minister of Jehovah God, commissioned to do his will.

Most of these ministers spend about fifteen hours a month spreading the word of Jehovah, although a minority—known as Pioneers—give more than seventy hours a month. House-to-house preaching is considered a Christlike and apostolic method of evangelism. Witnesses go from door to door, using their Bibles to speak with people on themes of particular interest to the hearer. They also distribute literature containing Bible-based articles and items of current interest.

Use of the Bible

The Witnesses make extensive use of the Bible. Quoting from scripture, they use numerous proof texts from scattered portions of the Bible to validate their beliefs. For example, Genesis 9:4, which prohibits eating meat with the blood in it, and Acts 15:28-29, instructing the Christians in Antioch to "abstain . . . from blood," are employed to prove that blood transfusions are wrong. Ecclesiastes 9:5, 10, verses that describe the unconscious state of the dead, and Acts 17:31, Paul's words regarding the hope of a future resurrection, are used to show that the dead are in the grave awaiting their resurrection to life.

A major teaching of Jehovah's Witnesses emphasizes the apocalyptic passages of the Bible dealing with the end of the present "system of things" and the restoration of paradise on the earth.

Meeting in Halls

Witnesses gather in private homes or modest auditoriums called Kingdom Halls to study the Bible and equip themselves for preaching the kingdom's message. The name Kingdom Hall puts emphasis on what Witnesses see as their main purpose: to advertise God's kingdom as the hope of the world.

Congregations are kept small. When one reaches about two hundred members, the members form two congregations. The congregation schedules five meetings each week that include instruction in the Bible, doctrine, and public speaking.

The Kingdom Hall is seen as the center of pure worship. Any Witness who willfully and unrepentantly does not live up to Bible standards, for example, by living an immoral life, consistently getting drunk, or habitually stealing, may be "disfellowshiped."

Instruction is also given at annual conventions. Smaller ones of one thousand to two thousand Witnesses in a local area are called circuit assemblies, and larger conventions of five thousand to twenty thousand or more, called district conventions, may be national or international in scope.

Origins of the Society

Witnesses claim to follow no individual person. The founder and first president of the Watch Tower Society, Charles Taze Russell, was a layperson who gathered a group of people around him for Bible study. His guiding idea was to use the Bible as the only standard and its teachings as the only creed. Russell's group grew, and by 1878 he was leader of an independent congregation. He was a prolific writer and began publishing *The Watchtower* magazine in 1879. Early in the next century, the group adopted the name "Jehovah's Witnesses," from Isaiah 43:10, "You are my witnesses." Previously, they used the name Bible Students or were called by such names as Russellites or Millennial Dawnites.

Doctrinally Different

Unlike most groups that claim to follow the Christian tradition, the Witnesses do not hold to the doctrine of the Trinity. They refer to Jesus as the Son of God, not God the Son, and he is considered to be subject to God, the Father, being a creation of Jehovah God. They believe that Jesus was not resurrected in a fleshly body but ascended into heaven with a spirit body after his death. Christ's life course on earth is seen as an example that Christians strive to follow.

Emphasis is placed on the coming rule of God's kingdom over the earth, with Jesus Christ as its heavenly king. Christ is believed to have "returned" spiritually in 1914, when he began ruling in heaven as king of God's kingdom.

Witnesses believe that through his death as a perfect man on earth, Jesus provided the ransom and opened the way for humans to be delivered from the sin and death that all have inherited because of the sin of humankind's forefather Adam.

Because Witnesses believe that accurate knowledge about God is essential, they print and distribute Bibles and Bible literature internationally. Their official journal, *The Watchtower*, has a circulation of approximately 22,300,000 in 130 languages.

Attitudes toward the World

Witnesses assert that the present corrupt system of things will be destroyed by God's hand during the "great tribulation," which includes the battle of Armageddon (Matthew 24:21; Revelation 7:14). Only then can paradise be restored to earth.

Witnesses do not take part in interfaith movements. They carefully examine the doctrines of various churches and consider false any unscriptural aspects of those teachings.

Because their allegiance is to God first, Witnesses maintain strict political neutrality and therefore do not bear arms in warfare or participate in the affairs of government. They respect national flags, but because they view saluting as an act of worship, they do not salute the flag of any nation. Witnesses claim to give their worship and allegiance only to God, but they affirm strict adherence to all human laws that do not conflict with God's.

Seeking to follow the pattern of the early Christians, Witnesses maintain and publish their convictions throughout the world. They view this as an urgent task, for they believe Armageddon is close and the kingdom is at hand.

For Discussion

1. Both Lutherans and Jehovah's Witnesses claim to base their beliefs on the Bible. Why, then, do you think there are such striking differences in their doctrines?

2. Because Jehovah's Witnesses hold beliefs that are different from historic Christian beliefs, some question whether Jehovah's Witnesses should be considered Christian. What criteria do you think should be used to decide?

3. A centerpiece of Witness activity is proclaiming their beliefs from house to house. Do you think all Christians should do more of that? Why or why not?

For Further Study

· The following materials are published by the Watch Tower Bible and Tract Society of Pennsylvania and can be downloaded at the Jehovah's Witnesses website, www.jw.org:
  - *The Watchtower*
  - *What Does the Bible Really Teach?*
  - *Good News from God*

· *Apocalypse Delayed: The Story of Jehovah's Witnesses*, 3rd ed., by M. James Penton (University of Toronto Press, 2015)

· Jehovah's Witnesses website: www.jw.org

Table of Comparison

	Jehovah's Witnesses	Lutherans
Teachings	1. Reject the Trinity. Only Jehovah is worshiped as creator and God almighty. 2. Believe that Christ was the first creation by God. 3. Believe in a future opportunity for salvation for those who do not have such opportunity in this life. 4. Reject the idea of eternal torment for the wicked. Evil souls are annihilated.	1. Accept the triune nature of God—Father, Son, and Holy Spirit. The name "Jehovah" is a mistaken combination of Hebrew consonants and vowels. 2. Accept the divinity of Christ, the Son of God from all eternity. 3. Believe humankind's eternal destiny is determined in this life. 4. Accept the reality of judgment as taught by the scriptures.
Type of Worship	No liturgy. Services largely consist of Bible study and sermons. Children learn and worship with adults. No Sunday school.	Liturgical pattern of worship used. Seek to nurture faith through worship and other programs.
Governance	Oversight by a governing body. Congregations supervised by local body of elders. No clergy/laity distinctions.	Interdependent congregational, regional, national, and global expressions of the church are characterized by democratic decision making, strong ecumenical relationships, elected leadership, and an ordained ministry.
Statistics*	Membership: 1,186,598 Congregations: 13,871	

*Figures reported in *2015 Yearbook of Jehovah's Witnesses*, pp. 178–87, published by the Watch Tower and Tract Society of Pennsylvania, the main legal entity for Jehovah's Witnesses.

CHAPTER 20

JUDAISM

The lighting of the nine-branch candelabra on Hanukkah symbolizes God's faithfulness to the Jewish people.

Judaism is not merely another faith tradition among the many world religions. Most Jews today say that being Jewish is more a matter of ancestry or culture than religion, and surveys consistently show that about 40 percent of Jewish adults are affiliated—that is, they belong (pay dues) to a synagogue or other Jewish organization or have a child in Jewish education. In addition, faith is less important to Judaism than practice. If we define Judaism solely—or even primarily—as a religious faith, we lose sight of those who are "secular," who accept the label "Jew" but who do not participate in synagogue worship or home ritual. The terms *Jew* and *Judaism* are themselves relatively modern and cannot be applied to any scriptural description of Hebrews, Israelites, and Judeans.

Still, Judaism is the source from which almost all Western faiths developed. It includes many facets, all of them overlapping. The only statement all Jews can agree on is this: all Jews believe in only one God. A full description of contemporary Jews must take into account the following:

· a monotheistic religious identity that draws on its roots in sacred scripture;
· a rabbinic tradition of ongoing interpretation;
· a diverse history of experiences of living among other, dominant cultures;
· a complex literature of lore, law, and ritual practice;
· a modern national identity linked to a specific land and culture; and finally,
· God, Torah, and Israel.

God, Torah, and Israel

The following terms describe or define Jews and Judaism as a faith perspective. Each requires further development, especially in interfaith dialogue.

The concepts of God, Torah, and Israel are essential in any definition of Jews and Judaism. *God* is the creator of the universe, the redeemer from Egyptian slavery as well as the source of ultimate redemption, and the revealer of those teachings and laws that constitute the Torah, the word of God's presence. The *Torah* is the five books of Moses (Genesis through Deuteronomy) as revealed on Mount Sinai and remains the primary source for the still-expanding literature of rabbinic interpretations of ritual behavior, theology, and ethics. *Israel* describes both the actual community of people from biblical times to the present and the physical geo-political-cultural land of Israel.

Humankind is the purposeful creation of God. From the time of Abraham through the present, Jews understand themselves to be in a covenant relationship with God. In this covenant, both personal and transcendent, the opportunity to engage in the observance of *mitzvot*—commandments—links Jews as individuals within a community to God.

Scripture provides the initial *mitzvot* (traditionally 613 commandments are counted, while Christians generally think of only ten) that are continually interpreted by rabbinic authority in every age. Thus, while scripture provides the initial commandments, it is the rabbinic interpretation, from the third century until the present, that defines the specific behavior, such as Sabbath observance, wedding ceremonies, ethical guides, and liturgical services.

Of all the foundational ideas, Israel is the most complex to explain. The Jewish community encompasses varied ethnic and cultural differences: *Ashkenazi* Jews come from Central and Eastern Europe and make up the vast majority of Jews with whom most readers will engage. *Sephardi* Jews are Western European, Spanish, North African, and native-born Israelis. Each of these major categories has many separate specific dialects, rituals, and liturgical identities. Israel is also the modern nation-state established in 1948 and has its own independent language, culture, history, and religious/political environment.

It is important to understand that not all Israelis are Jews, and not all Jews are connected to the State of Israel. In addition, the Israelites in scripture have nothing to do with today's Israelis. Nor do the Jews depicted in, say, *Fiddler on the Roof* (United Artists, 1971) or *Schindler's List* (Universal Pictures, 1993) have anything to do with either the Hebrews or Jews described in most Hebrew or Christian scripture. One must be very careful to determine what the term *Jew* means in each instance.

Holy Time

Judaism has a rich weekly and annual calendar. The holiest day in the Jewish calendar is *Shabbat*, the Sabbath, which begins on Friday night at sundown and concludes on Saturday at sundown. The Sabbath is linked to both the creation of the universe and the exodus from Egypt. Jews traditionally initiate the Sabbath as well as other holy days by lighting at least two candles and saying a blessing over wine or grape juice and bread (*challah* in Hebrew). This Sabbath home meal is understood to be a very significant family and communal religious experience. Synagogue services are held Friday evening and Saturday morning.

The fall cycle of holy days, the dates based on the Jewish lunar calendar, begins with *Rosh Hashanah* (New Year), continues with the Ten Days of Repentance, and then concludes with *Yom Kippur* (Day of Atonement). These are called the High Holy Days. *Sukkot* (the Feast of Tabernacles) begins on the fifth day after Yom Kippur, runs for seven to eight days, and concludes with *Simchat Torah* (Rejoicing with the Torah). *Hanukkah*, the Feast of Lights, commemorates a military victory by the Judeans over the Assyrian Greeks in the year 165 BCE. Legend has it that when the temple was rededicated, there was not enough consecrated oil to light the candelabra or menorah, but a small amount miraculously lasted eight days. This miracle is remembered every year by lighting a nine-branch candelabra, *hanukiah*. This festival does not have religious value comparable to Christmas, though both occur at the winter solstice. *Purim*, a festival based on the book of Esther, is usually midwinter and commemorates the reversal of a national threat to Jewish survival.

Pesach, or Passover, is probably the most observed home festival and includes the Seder meal and retelling of the exodus story in the *Haggadah*. During the seven to eight days of the festival, Jews do not eat any leavening but rather *matzah* and other special Passover food. Passover is fundamentally linked to Easter. Although scholars debate the nature of the connection, tradition holds that the last supper was a Seder meal shared by Jesus and his disciples, all of whom were Jews. It has become relatively common for churches to host a Seder to connect with this Jewish ritual in which some Christian rituals are rooted. *Shavuot*, Pentecost, is the late spring or early summer festival that remembers the giving of the Torah at Mount Sinai and completes the cycle of pilgrimage festivals noted in scripture: *Sukkot, Pesach, Shavuot*. Today most non-Orthodox contemporary Jews observe Shavuot as a significant public completion of Jewish education (tenth grade) linked to the giving of the Torah.

All of these holy days have specific rituals and liturgies as well as distinctive symbols. Like most contemporary Christians, Jews participate in services most intensely during the High Holy Days (much like Christmas and Easter) and for certain Sabbath observances. Two observances that link Jews to their modern history are *Yom HaShoah* (Holocaust Memorial Day) and *Yom Ha'atzmaut* (Israeli Independence Day), although celebration of these days is not widespread.

Jewish History

Scripture begins with creation, and thus Jews trace their history in the "universal" (before the chosen people were identified) first eleven chapters of Genesis. Judaism's particular history begins with God's call to Abraham in Genesis 12 and continues through the scriptural narratives, Prophets, and finally the Writings (Psalms, Proverbs, Job, and so forth). Thus, the first element of Jewish history is biblical and concludes with 168 BCE, in the time of the Greek domination and Hanukkah.

From 168 BCE to 1000 CE is the rabbinic period, during which the great interpretative texts of Jewish law and lore were developed, written, and edited. This is the first great period of Diaspora Jewry, the dispersion of Jews throughout the world after the Romans destroyed the temple in 70 CE. The texts reflect Jews adapting to non-Jewish cultures and the development of rabbis—teachers—in place of a priesthood and sacrifices in the temple. The *Mishnah* (assembled around 200 CE) and then the *Gemara* (500 CE) together make up the great body of Jewish law called the *Talmud*, which continues to influence how Judaism is practiced. Later legal texts are interpretations and commentaries of these primary texts. During this period several *midrashim*—sermonic interpretations—were also produced, several of which represent the mystical strain of Judaism.

The medieval period (1000–1650 CE) is primarily a history of Jewish relations with the dominant cultures and religions of Christianity and Islam. The literature becomes more philosophical, featuring such luminaries as Maimonides and Halevi. During this period a great deal of material reflects the tormented relationship between Judaism and Christianity. Any careful examination of Jews and Judaism must examine the centuries of contempt between these two faiths. Jews were expelled from every Christian country in Europe except Holland and the Scandinavian countries. This history of mistrust and persecution is the foundation for many of the issues Jews are still trying to understand and forgive today.

Finally, the modern period (1650 CE to the present) is about Jews moving throughout Europe and eventually North America and their creative adaptation to the Enlightenment. The movements of Judaism—Reform, Orthodox, Conservative, and Reconstructionist—are all products of this period of immigration and acculturation. One can trace liberal and rational movements, then a reaction emphasizing tradition, another reaction seeking a midpoint between liberal and traditional Judaism as experienced in America, and finally a contemporary attempt to bridge the liberal and the traditional. Each movement has its own ideologies, liturgies, communal authorities, seminaries, and publications, but all share the basics of Judaism as described above. Most large cities have temples (Reform), synagogues (Conservative), and shuls (Orthodox) to which guests are welcome, and many rabbis are willing to engage in dialogue with Christian churches.

The two most extraordinary events of contemporary Jewish history are the Holocaust and the establishment of the State of Israel. The destruction of six million Jews in Europe is fundamental to any sense of identity for a Jew today. Jews do not deny that another 5.2 million non-Jews were also killed, but the Holocaust is a unique act of genocide that should not be trivialized by comparing it to other horrible acts of mass destruction.

The establishment of Israel as a Jewish homeland has also had a transforming impact on Jewish identity. For the first time since the destruction of the temple and the beginning of the Diaspora, Jews can choose to live in a country ruled by and for a Jewish majority. The difference between the religious and cultural Jewish identity in Israel and in the rest of the world Jewish community is immense and is a source of great struggle within the Jewish community. The current political power of ultra-Orthodox Jews in the Israeli parliament has created a dangerous division among world Jewry and confuses non-Jewish Americans for whom such religious wars ended long ago. No understanding of contemporary Jews and Judaism is possible without considering what it means for Jews to live after Auschwitz and in the presence of a vibrant Jewish state.

Life Cycles

Like all faith communities, Jews have specific ritual acts marking occasions from birth through death, but these are merely family and personal occasions for private and communal celebration, not sacraments or sacramentals. There are significant differences among the movements of Judaism, especially related to gender equality and, most recently, sexual orientation. These differences reflect the attempts by Jews and Judaism to adapt to the challenges of the twenty-first century.

· *Bris*, baby naming: On the eighth day after birth, a male child is circumcised by a *mohel* (a person qualified to circumcise) and given a Hebrew name. The origin of the ceremony is Genesis 15. Many communities now name baby girls on the eighth day in a ceremony of covenant.

· *Bar/Bat (Bas) Mitzvah* is a public ceremony celebrated when a boy or girl reaches the age of 13 and is considered for ritual purposes an adult in the Jewish community. During the ceremony, which takes place most commonly in a temple or synagogue on Sabbath morning, the teen leads the worship service and reads from the Torah scroll and then teaches what he or she has learned. The ceremony culminates several years of learning Hebrew and scripture, although it does not originate in scripture or rabbinic literature. Many Reform, Conservative, and Reconstructionist congregations have a ceremony called "confirmation" that was borrowed from Lutheran churches in Germany. Confirmation today marks older teens' completion of a phase of religious education.

· The Jewish wedding ceremony is a public act in which the two people exchange vows under a *chupah*, a wedding canopy, after signing a *ketubah*, a wedding contract, in front of two witnesses. According to Jewish law, no rabbi is required, though by modern convention the rabbi acts on behalf of the civil authority. The particularity of a Jewish wedding is highlighted in the final phrase of the vows, *kedat moshe v'israel*, "according to the law of Moses and Israel." Intermarriage between Jews and non-Jews is a significant issue in the Jewish community. Some rabbis believe this vow in the service does not allow for an interfaith wedding service and that blending Jewish and Christian ritual is inappropriate. These rabbis argue that such couples should accept the differences that define their faith communities and have a civil ceremony, affirming the truths of both Judaism and Christianity.

· The rituals for mourning among Jews are extensive. Basic elements include a funeral during which psalms and modern readings are recited and a eulogy given, followed by burial in the ground, usually in a wooden coffin in a consecrated Jewish cemetery. For seven days following the funeral, the family "sits *shiva*" at home, accepting visits and holding services in the evening. Many non-Orthodox observe this ritual for three days. At the end of one year, the headstone/grave marker is dedicated. On the anniversary of the death—*yahrzeit*—the name of the deceased is read during services, and the mourners rise to say *Kaddish*, the mourners' prayer.

For Discussion

1. In what ways can you tell that Christianity developed out of the Jewish faith?

2. How has this article helped you to distinguish between the Jews or Israelites of the Bible and modern Jews?

3. In what ways does our society assume people are Christian? How can avoiding this assumption make our lives richer?

For Further Study

· *Living Judaism: The Complete Guide to Jewish Belief, Tradition, and Practice* by Wayne D. Dosick (HarperOne, 2010)

· *A Short History of the Jewish People: From Legendary Times to Modern Statehood* (Oxford University Press, 2000)

· *What Is a Jew?* by Morris N. Kertzer (Touchstone, 1996)

· Websites
  - Jewish Reconstructionist Communities: www.jewishrecon.org
  - Union for Reform Judaism: www.reformjudaism.org
  - United Synagogue of Conservative Judaism: www.uscj.org
  - Union of Orthodox Jewish Congregations of America: www.ou.org

Table of Comparison

	Judaism	*Lutherans*
Teachings	1. Believe the everlasting covenant between God and Israel is rooted in God's love. The Torah reveals God's will for the people and is obeyed by the people in faith as their part in the covenant.	1. Believe that since humanity rebelled against God, God sent Jesus into the world to establish a new covenant, so all people might believe and be saved.
	2. Accept the Torah is the complete guide for Jewish life. This may refer to all Jewish writings, the Hebrew Bible (Old Testament), or the Pentateuch (first five books of the Bible).	2. Accept the Bible (Old and New Testaments) as the written witness to God's revelation of saving action through Jesus Christ. Jesus Christ is the key to interpreting the Bible.
	3. Teach that beings are created good and in the likeness of God. They are able to fulfill God's will by living according to the Torah. Sin is a human action that violates God's will.	3. Teach that beings were created good and in the likeness of God but are by nature sinful as a consequence of the fall. Sin is a condition that can be overcome only through Jesus Christ.
Type of Worship	Worship is centered in the home and synagogue. The synagogue is a place of prayer, learning, and social activity.	Worship is centered in the church. The church defines itself as the community where the gospel is proclaimed and the sacraments administered.

Governance	Reform congregations are autonomous; Conservative and Orthodox congregations are subject to the rules and principles of their movements. Congregations are led by an ordained rabbi(s) and an elected board of laypeople.	Interdependent congregational, regional, national, and global expressions of the church are characterized by democratic decision making, strong ecumenical relationships, elected leadership, and an ordained ministry.

Statistics*

Union for Reform Judaism

Membership	288,580	Houses of worship	834

Union of Orthodox Jewish Congregations of America

Membership	256,303	Houses of worship	1,915

United Synagogue of Conservative Judaism

Membership	200,683	Houses of worship	599

Jewish Reconstructionist Federation

Membership	16,774	Houses of worship	98

*Figures estimated and reported by Steven M. Cohen and Jonathon Ament in *2010 ARDA Jewish Congregation Data*, Association of Religion Data Archives (ARDA), http://www.bjpa.org/Publications/details.cfm?PublicationID=21934.

CHAPTER 21

LUTHERAN CHURCH—MISSOURI SYNOD

Martin Luther's translation of scripture into the language of the people (German) laid a foundation for the LCMS view that the Bible teaches the one way of salvation in Jesus Christ.

The Lutheran Church—Missouri Synod (LCMS) has always taken its confession of faith seriously. Such confessional seriousness prompted a determined group to leave its homeland in Germany when it became convinced that the unhindered expression of Lutheran teaching was no longer possible in its native Saxony, where rationalism prevailed. Risking everything, approximately 750 Lutherans crossed the Atlantic in 1838 under the direction of Martin Stephan. Four of five ships arrived safely in New Orleans. A year later the fledgling group traveled up the Mississippi River and settled in Perry County, Missouri (south of St. Louis).

Trauma soon followed. Stephan, the group's esteemed leader, was charged with sexual immorality and was expelled from the community. The leadership vacuum was filled by young C. F. W. Walther (1811–1887), who emerged as the theological spokesperson for the disillusioned group, which was struggling to regain its spiritual and doctrinal bearings in an entirely foreign cultural setting. Finally, after a time of intense study and debate, and then after years of communication with other North American Lutherans, the German Evangelical Lutheran Synod of Missouri, Ohio, and Other States was born in 1847 with twelve congregations and about thirty-five hundred members. Walther would be its preeminent teacher and pastor, whether officially or otherwise, for four decades. The adjective "German" remained until World War I, as Missouri retained its ethnic identity longer than most American Lutheran groups. The name was finally shortened in 1947 to the Lutheran Church—Missouri Synod.

The Missouri Synod's efforts led to numerical growth, most dramatically during the latter part of the nineteenth century and the first half of the twentieth century. Today the LCMS has about 2.3 million members in approximately six thousand congregations. Its educational system numbers nearly 2,165 early childhood and elementary schools, more than ninety high schools, a ten school university system, and two seminaries. Geographically, the Missouri Synod is strongest in the midwestern United States.

Doctrine and Life

The doctrine and practice of the Missouri Synod have been built on an uncompromising affirmation of biblical authority and truthfulness and a conscientious commitment to the sixteenth-century Lutheran Confessions. At the center of scripture and at the core of the confessional writings is God's justification of the ungodly by grace, for the sake of Jesus Christ, through faith—all without any human preparation or cooperation. (The Confessions include the Apostles', Nicene, and Athanasian Creeds; the Augsburg Confession and its Apology; Luther's Small and Large Catechisms; the Smalcald Articles and the Treatise on the Power and Primacy of the Pope; and the Formula of Concord.)

From the days of Walther to the present—and again following the emphases of Martin Luther, Philip Melanchthon, and the other confessional authors—the Missouri Synod has emphasized law and gospel as the two principal teachings into which scripture is divided. The law exposes human sinfulness, while the gospel is God's definitive and final promise of forgiveness, life, and salvation to those who are broken and helpless in the face of the law's indictment. The message of salvation is communicated to sinners through the spoken word of absolution and through the sacraments of baptism and the Lord's supper, which give the basic structure to the Lutheran liturgy. Through these means of grace alone, the triune God creates and sustains the church, which in turn can be recognized by the presence of this same quickening word and these two sacraments. The Missouri Synod sees the "body of doctrine" as an organic whole that is unified and informed by the gospel, and it views the entire Bible, both the Old and New Testaments, as teaching one way of salvation in Jesus Christ.

The Missouri Synod has been characterized by a polity of congregational interdependence, a commitment to Christian education at all levels (and especially at the elementary school level—its school system being perhaps its best-known feature among those otherwise unfamiliar with the Missouri Synod's doctrine and practice), diligent pastoral care, invitations to pursue unity with other like-minded American Lutherans, innovative and varied evangelism efforts, and extensive overseas missions.

Shaped by Controversy

The history of the Missouri Synod has not been without controversy. In its earliest years, Walther helped the infant community work through issues pertaining to the doctrines of church and ministry. On the basis of scripture, the Lutheran Confessions, and especially the writings of Martin Luther, Walther was able both to reassure the Saxons of their churchly identity and to preserve the balance between the divine institution of the pastoral office and the rights and privileges of the priesthood of all believers. Near the turn of the twentieth century, Walther and then his successor, Francis Pieper, wrote extensively on the doctrine of God's eternal election, stressing not only that salvation is from beginning to end God's accomplishment in Jesus Christ, but also that God had chosen God's children in Christ from eternity.

Just as the controversy over election helps explain alliances among American Lutheran groups at the turn of the twentieth century, so the configuration of American Lutheranism today is in part a consequence of the most serious controversy the Missouri Synod faced during the 1960s and 1970s. From the Missouri Synod's perspective (and vastly oversimplified), this debate focused on the authority and interpretation of the Bible. "Biblical criticism" (in which the biblical text is analyzed using sophisticated scholarly methods applicable to any other literature) had become fairly common in several other American Lutheran church bodies, and by the 1960s it was appearing in Missouri Synod classrooms and pulpits. For some people in the synod, biblical criticism compromised the truthfulness of scripture and potentially undermined the historical foundations of the gospel itself. Others argued that this perspective was a misunderstanding. They regarded the so-called historical-critical method as a neutral tool that could, if used properly, aid in biblical interpretation.

A complicated sequence of events reached a climax in 1973 and 1974: the doctrinal position of the majority of the Concordia Seminary (St. Louis) faculty was condemned, Concordia's president was suspended, the same faculty and most students declined to continue their work under a new administration, and eventually the faculty majority and president were dismissed.

The events at Concordia Seminary had their counterparts in other areas and agencies of the synod. Sadly, all efforts at conciliation failed. In 1976 approximately 225 congregations and roughly 4 percent of its total membership left the Missouri Synod to form the Association of Evangelical Lutheran Churches, which would become part of the Evangelical Lutheran Church in America in 1988. (The LCMS itself has never been part of a major merger.)

How Much Agreement?

These more recent controversies color the landscape of American Lutheran relations down to the present day. The initial debates of the 1960s and 1970s have given rise to another cluster of issues, especially to the question of how much agreement is necessary before Christians can worship and celebrate the sacraments together. The Missouri Synod sees its confession of faith as requiring agreement in "the gospel in all its articles" (following the principle of one of the confessional writings noted earlier, the Formula of Concord). In the eyes of many in the Missouri Synod, their sisters and brothers in the ELCA seem to maintain that basic agreement in the gospel and a less comprehensive doctrinal confession is sufficient. Indeed, as an LCMS past president observed, the Missouri Synod and the ELCA disagree about the significance of disagreeing.

The LCMS continues to address issues of confessional identity. Internal conflict did not end with the difficulties of the 1970s. Perhaps the most challenging issue facing this church today is the basic question of what it means to be a confessional Lutheran church body in an age when American Christians seem increasingly less denominationally conscious or concerned.

At its best, the LCMS seeks to keep the gospel central in its total congregational life, its mission work across the globe, its educational institutions, and its deliberative assemblies. It aspires to be faithful and attentive to holy scripture, from which alone it hears God's announcement of forgiveness in Jesus Christ. Finally, it strives to echo the evangelical confession of faith made by its sixteenth-century forebears in the *Book of Concord*. Its history is not an unbroken success story; nevertheless, it is a story beyond anything a struggling group of immigrants could ever have imagined.

For Discussion

1. From what you know, where would you stand on the question of how to interpret the Bible?

2. How much agreement do you think should be necessary before people can worship together? Before they can take communion together?

For Further Study

· *Heritage in Motion: Readings in the History of the Lutheran Church—Missouri Synod*, ed. August Suelflow (Concordia, 2011)

· *Lutheranism 101*, ed. Scot A. Kinnaman and Laura L. Lane (Concordia, 2010)

· Lutheran Church—Missouri Synod website: www.lcms.org

Table of Comparison

	Lutheran Church—Missouri Synod	Evangelical Lutheran Church in America
Teachings	1. Believe in the triune God—Father, Son, and Holy Spirit.	1. Same.
	2. Accept the Lutheran Confessions as true teachings of biblical faith.	2. Same.
	3. Believe that God comes to us through the word and the sacraments of baptism and holy communion.	3. Same.
	4. Teach justification by grace through faith.	4. Same.
	5. Believe that the Bible should not be subjected to higher critical methods.	5. Believe that the Bible can speak effectively through the use of higher critical study methods.
	6. Believe that the Bible restricts women from certain church positions, including ordained ministry.	6. Believe that the Bible permits, even encourages, full participation by women in the life of the church.
	7. Consider a high degree of doctrinal agreement necessary before fellowship is possible.	7. Consider agreement on a more basic level sufficient for fellowship.
Type of Worship	Mostly liturgical, following the classical form of the Western church.	Same.
Governance	Congregational form with some supervision at district and national levels.	Interdependent congregational, synodical, regional, and national "expressions."
Statistics	Membership: 2,270,921 Congregations: 6,040	

CHAPTER 22

MENNONITE CHURCH

The Amish, one branch of Mennonites, meet for worship in homes rather than church buildings.

On any Sunday you will find Mennonites gathered for worship in about eighty countries around the world. They now number more than one million, and more than half live in Africa, Asia, and South America. Mennonites are multicultural, with a wide variety of practices and people: from a "plain" Pennsylvania farmer to a California university professor; from an African American businesswoman to a Hispanic physician; from an African community leader to a South American sociologist.

Mennonites trace their beginnings to the sixteenth-century Protestant Reformation in Europe. A small group of believers were convinced that Martin Luther and Ulrich Zwingli had not gone far enough in their reforms. Conrad Grebel, son of an important Swiss family, led this group, which attempted to recover New Testament Christianity. They baptized one another at Zurich, Switzerland, in January 1525, thus sparking a more radical reformation called the Anabaptist movement.

These believers were called Anabaptists by their opponents because they rejected infant baptism and re- (*ana* in Greek) baptized adults. By rejecting infant baptism, they defied the state-church authorities and found themselves considered heretics. They were hunted down and killed as enemies of God and the state. Thousands died as martyrs by burning, beheading, or drowning. Accounts of their suffering and death were recorded in *Martyrs Mirror*, a collection of stories that continue to be retold. Though Anabaptists were hunted and killed, most refused to use the sword, even in self-defense. They read the Bible through the lens of the Sermon on the Mount and thus followed Jesus' call to practice nonviolent love and mutual aid.

Persecution scattered the Anabaptists throughout Europe. Because of their zealous evangelism, the movement spread rapidly. In the Netherlands, a Catholic priest named Menno Simons (from whose name comes *Mennonites*) joined the movement in 1536. He became an evangelist and shepherd of the scattered Anabaptists in the Netherlands and north Germany. Though a reward of 100 guilders was offered for his capture, Simons avoided arrest and served the movement for twenty-five years.

While Mennonites were first tolerated in the Netherlands, where some became wealthy, persecution continued in other parts of Western Europe. Mennonites emigrated to North America beginning in 1681.

Amish and Hutterites

Hutterites and Amish were part of the original Anabaptist movement. The Hutterites trace their origin to Jacob Hutter, who died a martyr in Austria in 1536. The group emphasized the importance of sharing material possessions as a sign of love and grace. They have established many self-sufficient colonies in Canada and the northern United States. The Hutterites use all available modern machinery but stress nonconformity to culture in dress and attitude, based on texts such as 1 John 2:15a, "Do not love the world or the things in the world."

The Amish arose out of efforts to address a problem all Christians face: trying to follow Christ in a sinful world. In 1693 Jacob Amman broke with the Swiss Mennonites when he called for stronger church discipline and greater separation from the world. To this day the Amish refuse to conform to their surrounding culture, dressing in seventeenth-century garb, refusing to use cars or other modern machinery, and meeting in homes rather than church buildings for worship.

Emphasis on the Bible

Mennonites believe in the inspiration of the entire Bible, looking to the Old Testament to discern God's way with people of old and to the New Testament as a guide for faith and life today. They have no objection to the Apostles' Creed and use it occasionally in their worship services. The ordinances of baptism and the Lord's supper are understood as symbolic acts that recall the finished work of Christ and prepare the believer for a life of obedience and discipleship. All people who are going to be baptized first give an oral statement of faith to the congregation.

Mennonites believe that Christian living means participating in Christ's work in the world. This means being ready to suffer. It means taking seriously Jesus' words in the Sermon on the Mount (Matthew 5–7), believing that it is possible to obey Jesus' commandments today. Mennonites also use the Bible as a guide for the kind of congregations they build. They believe that every member has been given gifts by the Holy Spirit to use for the common good (1 Corinthians 12). Consequently, the central task of the pastor is to help equip every member to minister to his or her greatest potential.

With other Christians, Mennonites believe that human beings are sinners in need of redemption. But people are not born with sin; rather, it is a problem of the will. This means that children are innocent of sin until they have reached the age when they can know right from wrong and the long-range implications of their actions. Then children are accountable for their sins.

Service throughout the World

North American Mennonites began organizing home and foreign missions in the late 1800s. They first sent missionaries overseas during the years 1899–1915, and another round of mission expansion followed World War II.

To coordinate their relief and service programs, Mennonites organized the Mennonite Central Committee (MCC) in 1920. The Mennonite World Conference was founded in 1925 for fellowship with the global church.

With love as the primary motive, Mennonites seek to serve others at their point of need—discrimination, war, or poverty—knowing that God is the Lord of history and that they are called to be God's helpers in the world. God's rule will be perfect on earth only when Christ returns.

For Discussion

1. Many Mennonites make visible their separateness from the world. What do you think of that as a strategy for the Christian life?

2. What differences do you find between the Mennonite understanding of baptism and that of your church?

For Further Study

- *Beliefs: Mennonite Faith and Practice*, John Roth Trilogy, by John D. Roth (Herald, 2005)
- *Practices: Mennonite Worship and Witness*, John Roth Trilogy, by John D. Roth (Herald, 2009)
- *Stories: How Mennonites Came to Be*, John Roth Trilogy, by John D. Roth (Herald, 2006)
- Websites:
  - Beachy-Amish Mennonite Churches: www.beachyam.org
  - Church of God in Christ, Mennonite: churchofgodinchristmennonite.net
  - Conservative Mennonite Conference: www.cmcrosedale.org
  - Mennonite Church USA: mennoniteusa.org
  - US Mennonite Brethren: www.usmb.org

Table of Comparison

	Mennonites	Lutherans
Teachings	1. Accept the Bible as the guide for faith and life.	1. Accept the Bible as the written witness to God's revelation of saving action through Jesus Christ.
	2. Consider two ordinances—baptism and communion—to be signs and symbols.	2. Celebrate two sacraments—baptism and communion—as means of grace.
	3. Have voluntary church membership and no infant baptism.	3. Receive infants and adults into the church by baptism.
	4. Believe faith means obedience to Christ.	4. Proclaim justification by grace through faith.
	5. Believe in triune nature of God.	5. Same.
	6. Advocate nonviolent peacemaking.	6. Value peacemaking, but no defined position on peace and war is taken.
Type of Worship	Nonliturgical with sermon central; often shared preaching and prayers. Singing sometimes unaccompanied. Simple, functional architecture.	Liturgical with both word and sacrament emphasized. Rich musical heritage. Church architecture is often used to symbolize relationship with God.
Governance	Congregations are autonomous but participate in the Mennonite World Conference and other Mennonite conferences for fellowship.	Interdependent congregational, regional, national, and global expressions of the church are characterized by democratic decision making, strong ecumenical relationships, elected leadership, and an ordained ministry.
Statistics*	Membership: 229,110 Congregations: 1,686	

*Figures include fifteen Mennonite groups. The largest is the Mennonite Church USA with 127,363 members in 919 congregations. Another 1,755 undifferentiated Amish groups include 241,356 members.

CHAPTER 23

METHODIST CHURCH

The Methodist movement in America spread quickly through the preaching of circuit riders.

The United Methodist Church is a worldwide denomination that traces its roots to England, yet it has adapted well to the American culture. It grew in this country through the efforts of circuit riders, and today it continues to preach God's love among the many cultures that make up our society.

Formation of the Methodist Church

The Methodist movement started in the eighteenth century in England under the leadership of John Wesley, a clergyman of the Church of England. Wesley organized small societies of Christians outside the Church of England, primarily from laboring classes that were not at that time being reached by the church. He trained a large number of laymen as preachers who conducted preaching services, taught classes, and provided pastoral care.

The movement was transplanted to America and in 1784 was organized in Baltimore as the Methodist Episcopal Church. It spread quickly across the land through the preaching of circuit riders, who rode from place to place preaching the gospel. These early Methodists emphasized the importance of a definite experience of God's grace, a clear consciousness of their conversion, commitment to personal purity and integrity, and enthusiasm for spreading the gospel. Bishop Francis Asbury was the great leader in early America, riding some 270,000 miles back and forth across the country from 1771 to 1816, preaching sixteen thousand sermons, ordaining four thousand ministers, and conducting 224 meetings of preachers.

During this same period, two movements arose in Pennsylvania. One was the United Brethren in Christ, and the other movement was originally called the Evangelical Association and later the Evangelical Church. In 1946 these two groups merged to form the Evangelical United Brethren Church.

A sizable group in the Methodist Episcopal Church, determined to create a more democratic church structure, withdrew from it in 1830 and formed the Methodist Protestant Church. In 1844 to 1845, the remaining members of the original Methodist body in this country divided into northern and southern branches, but these three segments came back together in 1939 as the Methodist Church. The Methodist Church and the Evangelical United Brethren Church united in 1968. Each church made certain concessions on their structure and practices, and each benefited from the other. The resulting denomination was called the United Methodist Church.

Approach to Faith

John Wesley preached that the grace and love of God are available to all people—not just a select few. He also declared that God gives to every person the ability to choose the good. All will be saved who turn to God in repentance, faith, and trust. Wesley had in his early years a life-changing experience that he described by saying, "I felt my heart strangely warm. I felt I did trust in Christ, Christ alone for salvation." This experience was stimulated, he said, at a meeting in which a part of Martin Luther's *Commentary on the Epistle to the Romans* had been read.

United Methodists hold to the doctrine of the Trinity, affirming God as Father, as Son, and as Holy Spirit. God the creator shows loving care for all creatures. At the same time, God's judgment is real. Because God is righteous, sin and the tragic consequences of sin, both individual and social, cannot be ignored. God suffers when we do wrong but does not reject us, because mercy and grace are always a part of God's relationship with us.

United Methodists believe in Jesus Christ as Son of God and as savior, Lord, and master for all who accept his claim on their lives. Through Christ, God offers redemption to humankind, doing for us what we cannot do for ourselves, that is, bringing new life and hope out of our shattered efforts.

God continues to be present within the church and the life of the individual Christian through the Holy Spirit. The Holy Spirit is the comforter, the revealer of truth, and the convictor of sin, bringing healing and purification. God's Spirit is ever active in the world and in the church. God will not be confined to certain historical dogmas. The Spirit breaks down every barrier and every formulation of the faith claimed to be the only true expression of the church.

Humankind and Salvation

United Methodists affirm that it is not possible for human beings to understand themselves apart from their relationship to God. True meaning and purpose in life are grounded only in God. Without this foundation, it is impossible to fulfill God's purposes. When human beings are alienated from God, they are captive to sin and turn away from God, acting with cruelty, selfishness, and hardheadedness.

Methodists believe that human beings are responsible for their sins. People sin not because of Adam, but because they want their own way rather than God's way. While it is true that some situations in life are beyond human control, people are not robots. Human beings are creatures who must decide. Morality, Methodists would argue, is possible only in a situation where people can choose to say yes or no to worshiping God.

When people turn away from God in favor of their own selfish ends, only God can offer grace and forgiveness. Through Christ, a person is able to see his or her own transgression. Through Christ's death and resurrection, God does for people what they cannot do for themselves by bringing new life and hope.

Perfection in Christian Love

United Methodists believe that as Christians we can claim no merit because of what we do, but when God's love is within our hearts and lives, we will bring forth the fruits of faith—sometimes called "good works." We do not do good works to try to please God; we respond with good works because we love God and our fellow creatures. We cannot avoid showing our love in this way.

United Methodists follow—at least in theory—John Wesley's doctrine of Christian perfection. Wesley wrote, "Christian perfection is neither more nor less than pure love; love expelling sin, and governing both the heart and the life of the child of God." He believed that every Christian could experience this fullness of love. This doctrine has not always been at the forefront of Methodist teaching, but it is still part of the denomination's character.

Faith and Practice

Methodist churches emphasize preaching the message of the Bible. Preaching is a means of witnessing to Christ or explaining the Christian faith, bringing comfort and assurance to those under stress, and challenging and rebuking people when necessary. In many United Methodist churches, the sermon is considered the most important part of the worship service; however, it is increasingly considered one among several important aspects of worship.

There are two sacraments in United Methodist practice: baptism and the Lord's supper. People are made children of God through baptism. United Methodists allow any mode of baptism but usually practice sprinkling. They also practice infant baptism, believing that in it God declares love and concern for the child through the church. United Methodists believe in open communion; all are welcome who can honestly respond to the invitation to "truly and earnestly repent of your sins, and are in love and charity with your neighbors, and intend to lead a new life." They believe in the spiritual presence of Christ in the Lord's supper—as contrasted with the belief in a literal physical presence in the bread and wine.

United Methodists look to the Bible as the ground and guide of all Christian learning and living. Creeds are respected and regularly used by United Methodists, but are not considered standards by which to test orthodoxy or as final statements of faith. In official use are the Nicene Creed, the Apostles' Creed, two modern statements of faith, and the Confession of Faith of the former Evangelical United Brethren Church, prepared in 1946.

Social Concerns

The interest of United Methodists in all aspects of human life—personal and social—is based on the biblical concern for justice. They attend to the needs of people who are poor and oppressed, the spiritual and physical welfare of all, and the desire for peace and goodwill among people and nations.

For many years Methodist have operated hospitals, orphanages, social centers, homes for youth, and schools for those otherwise neglected. In more recent years, they have also established homes for older people, supported inner-city churches and parishes, and developed special ministries with minority groups.

The statement of Social Principles in the *Book of Discipline* addresses a wide variety of issues, including the natural world, the nurturing community (family, sexuality), the social community (ethnic minorities, women, children, alcohol and other drugs, medical experimentation), the economic community, the political community, and the world community.

In the Ecumenical Movement

The United Methodist Church, through the six original denominational strands that make up the church today, has a long history of involvement in the ecumenical movements beginning in the twentieth century. One of the most important contributions has been providing leadership through its pastors, bishops, and scholars. United Methodists also have always provided significant financial support for the many ecumenical activities in which they have participated, including the National Council of Churches of Christ and the World Council of Churches.

Structural Features

The United Methodist Church is an episcopal body, which means that bishops appoint pastors to their churches. Individual United Methodist churches consider themselves organic parts of the church as a whole—just as the various cells of one's physical body make up the body as a whole. The pastors of United Methodist churches are not members of the congregations they serve, but belong to one of the regional groups called annual conferences. There are five levels in the conference structure. The General Conference, the highest legislative body, meets every four years.

Composition of Membership

The United Methodist Church is found in almost every county in the United States. Members include people of every economic status, age, and ethnic group. Among denominations that are primarily white, it has the largest number of members who are African American, Native American, Hispanic, and Asian American. This diversity requires members of United Methodist churches to be open to a variety of cultural practices and perspectives.

United Methodists hold a wide range of theological views. The denomination includes people of conservative theological views, those of liberal views, and many in between. While individual believers may hold to their own theological convictions firmly, members are encouraged to be tolerant of those who hold different beliefs. Similarly, members subscribe to a broad spectrum of views on social issues—the use of natural resources, homosexuality, abortion, sexist language, God-language, welfare practices, and so on.

For Discussion

1. Do we have the ability, on our own, to turn toward God? Methodism would say yes; Lutheranism would say no. Which position do you favor, and why?

2. Historically, Methodists have emphasized holy living more than have Lutherans. What do you think are the benefits and drawbacks of stressing lifestyle?

3. Methodists have been less willing than some other denominations to be tied down to historic statements of faith. Do you think this stance is an advantage or a liability? Why?

For Further Study

· *Finding Our Way: Love and Law in the United Methodist Church* by Rueben P. Job et al. (Abingdon, 2014)

· *United Methodist Beliefs: A Brief Introduction* by William H. Willimon (Westminster John Knox, 2007)

· *United Methodist Questions, United Methodist Answers*, rev. ed., by Belton Joyner (Westminster John Knox, 2015)

· United Methodist Church website: www.umc.org

Table of Comparison

	Methodists	Lutherans
Teachings	1. Believe the Bible contains the word of God. 2. Teach justification by faith. 3. Consider baptism and holy communion not only symbolically, but also as signs of God's grace. 4. Teach that all people have the ability to choose the good and turn to God. 5. Believe the church should express its faith in concrete action in the affairs of the world.	1. Accept the Bible as the written witness to God's revelation of saving action through Jesus Christ. 2. Same. 3. Consider baptism and holy communion as God's means of conveying God's grace. 4. Teach that we can reject God, but only God's work brings us to faith. 5. Believe the church lives to preach the gospel and celebrate the sacraments, giving strength for service in the world.
Type of Worship	Formerly very free and emotional. Now moving toward more formal and sometimes highly liturgical patterns.	Liturgical, following the classical form of the Western church.
Governance	Episcopal, with bishop but no claim to apostolic succession. Congregations quite free within clearly defined parameters.	Interdependent congregational, regional, national, and global expressions of the church are characterized by democratic decision making, strong ecumenical relationships, elected leadership, and an ordained ministry.
Statistics	Membership: 9,860,653 Congregations: 33,323	

CHAPTER 24

MORAVIAN CHURCH

The Moravian Church began when a Bohemian priest and scholar, John Hus, was burned at the stake at the Council of Constance in 1415.

The Moravian Church is not a large denomination. In spite of its small size, however, it is one of the few worldwide denominations. Moravians claim that fellowship in Jesus Christ can transcend all differences, including those of political systems and ethnicity.

From earliest times, the Moravian Church has sought Protestant cooperation. Leaders in Bohemia (now part of the Czech Republic) made contact with Martin Luther during the German Reformation. At that time, there were already 175,000 Moravians. As a result of that contact, when the Moravian Church, known as the *Unitas Fratrum* (Unity of Brethren), published its confession of faith, Luther wrote the preface. This spirit of cooperation continued in America. Moravian leaders in early Pennsylvania sought to encourage Protestant unity. More recently, American Moravians were charter members of both the World and National Councils of Churches.

A Worldwide Unity

The Moravian Church has maintained a worldwide organization, called the Unity, since the eighteenth century. Today's Unity embraces nineteen independent provinces and missions on every major continent except Australia. Each Unity province is an independent church, but a Unity Synod held every seven years provides overall coordination and direction for the church in the world.

The fastest-growing segment of the worldwide Moravian Church today is in Tanzania. The church is also present in South Africa, Suriname, Guyana, the West Indies, and Central America, as well as in Europe, the United Kingdom, and North America. Moravians also work among the native people of Alaska and Labrador.

Hus and Zinzendorf

The Moravian Church began when a Bohemian priest and scholar, John Hus, was burned at the stake at the Council of Constance, an ecumenical council recognized by the Roman Catholic Church and held in 1415. After efforts to purify the church failed, Hus's followers were forced to organize their own body in 1457.

The Unity prospered for a time. It soon faced persecution, however, and seemed dead—but it was reborn. A little band of refugees from Bohemia came to a devout, pietistic German Lutheran's estate in 1721. Count Nicolaus von Zinzendorf permitted them to settle on his lands. Under Zinzendorf's leadership, they worshiped as Lutherans in the parish church. Other religiously dissatisfied people and refugees joined the community. But strife arose, and this community seemed in danger of falling apart.

Count Zinzendorf abandoned his tasks at court and gave his full time to the community. He and the elders conducted a house-to-house visitation for prayer and study, which built toward a climax on August 13, 1727. The Brethren, gathered in the parish church, experienced an outpouring of God's Spirit of such vitality that the direction of the community was changed, and it became a solid base for spreading the gospel throughout the world.

From Europe the church spread to many parts of the world, seeking to take its message of Jesus to those left out by society, including indigenous peoples and people enslaved by others. Today the makeup of the Moravian Church is about 80 percent black people; about 10 percent white people; and the remaining members, indigenous peoples.

Church and Sacraments

The Moravian Church recognizes the sacraments of baptism and holy communion. The usual form of baptism is sprinkling, and the church administers the sacrament in the name of the triune God (Father, Son, and Holy Spirit). The sacrament carries with it the responsibility of parents, child, and congregation.

Baptism is a sign of God's love toward us even before we can understand it and a sign of our becoming part of the family of God through Christ. Baptized children may receive communion after some preparation; however, practice varies from congregation to congregation. At confirmation (for a person baptized as an infant) or baptism (for someone baptized as an adult), the person makes a confession of faith.

In the Moravian understanding of holy communion, the believer participates in the unique act of a covenant with Christ as Savior and with other believers in Christ. The Moravian service of holy communion is a service of praise and prayer (with hymns sung as the elements are distributed to all communicants), fellowship (with the right hand of fellowship extended at the beginning and close of the service), and covenant with Christ and each other.

The Love Feast

Moravian worship varies widely; freedom is intended. Liturgies, composed of prayers, scripture verses, and hymn stanzas, are provided for all occasions. The Moravian Easter Morning liturgy, sometimes called a Moravian confession of faith, draws heavily on Luther's Small Catechism. Another Moravian tradition is a series of services during Holy Week in which the entire Passion narrative of the Gospels is read, interspersed with hymns. These liturgical forms are not intended to restrict creative expression. A unique practice is the love feast, a simple meal shared in church. In such services, as in the service for holy communion, much of the message is conveyed in the words of the large number of hymns sung.

Christian Living

Moravians emphasize Christian living. They focus not so much on a list of don'ts as on encouragement to live a life centered on Jesus Christ. The faithful Moravian lives for Christ, rejoices in Christ, and shows a spirit of love for others.

The Moravian Church emphasizes a warm experience of personal salvation and mission work. It sought to function within the state churches of Europe and to secure their support in taking the gospel abroad. It also witnessed the divisiveness of contrary doctrine. As a result, though conservative where the major doctrines (the Trinity and so forth) are concerned, it has consistently refused to define the fine points, such as what happens to the elements in holy communion. Such definition is left to the individual Christian.

Broadly evangelical, the Moravians have insisted on the principle "In essentials unity, in nonessentials liberty, in all things love." The chief characteristic of its doctrinal approach came from Zinzendorf, who said, "If I know Jesus, then I know all that I need to know about the Godhead."

Shape and Future

The ministry of the Moravian Church is grouped into three orders: deacon, presbyter, and bishop. The bishop is not a governmental figure but is chosen as a spiritual leader and pastor to pastors.

The future of the Moravian Church lies in its continued witness for Christ around the world. Growth in North America in recent years has come mainly through immigration of Moravians from Central America and the Caribbean to the United States and Canada.

For Discussion

1. In 1999 Moravians and the Evangelical Lutheran Church in America established a "full communion" relationship. Why did this make sense?

2. The Moravians are a worldwide church. How does this compare with your denomination?

3. What are the benefits and possible pitfalls of the principle "In essentials unity, in nonessentials liberty, in all things love"?

For Further Study

· *Count Zinzendorf and the Spirit of the Moravians* by Paul Wemmer (Xulon, 2013)

· *Jesus Still Lead On: An Introduction to Moravian Belief* by Craig D. Atwood (Moravian Church Interprovincial Board of Communication, 2004), available at www.moravian.org

· *A History of the Moravian Church* by J. E. Hutton (CreateSpace Independent Publishing Platform, 2013)

· Moravian Church website: www.moravian.org

Table of Comparison

	Moravians	Lutherans
Teachings	1. Accept major statements of faith of the early church as well as major confessions of Lutheran and Reformed traditions, including the Barmen Declaration of 1934, as valid expressions.	1. Accept the creeds, the Augsburg Confession, and Luther's Small Catechism as basic summaries of the faith. Recognize the remainder of the *Book of Concord* as a valid interpretation of the faith of the church.
	2. Emphasize Christ as the revelation of God.	2. Same.
	3. Affirm the inspiration of scripture, but much latitude here in interpretation.	3. Accept the Bible as the written witness to God's revelation of saving action through Jesus Christ.
	4. Practice baptism and holy communion, but define them only in biblical terms. Each believer interprets those terms.	4. Practice baptism and holy communion as means of God's grace. Affirm the real presence of Christ in communion.
	5. Believe in the necessity of individual regeneration and in salvation through Christ.	5. Teach that the baptized Christian lives in the covenant of his or her baptism, dying to sin and rising again to faith in Christ.
Type of Worship	Semi-liturgical. Liturgies are available for every type of need but are not compulsory. Celebrate the love feast.	Liturgical, following the classical form of the Western church.
Governance	"Conferential," with wide latitude given to congregations.	Interdependent congregational, regional, national, and global expressions of the church are characterized by democratic decision making, strong ecumenical relationships, elected leadership, and an ordained ministry.
Statistics	Membership: 38,672 Congregations: 163	

CHAPTER 25

PRESBYTERIAN CHURCH

The word presbyterian *indicates a form of organization and governance that is based on rule by elected elders as representatives of the people.*

The Presbyterian Church (U.S.A.) is the largest church body in the world with a presbyterian form of government. But it is only one of many denominations that can properly be called *presbyterian*, because that word refers to a type of church organization practiced by a number of groups. This system of organization will be described later in this chapter.

Tradition and Change

The *Book of Confessions* is the basic document of the Presbyterian confessional position. It contains the Nicene Creed, the Apostles' Creed, the Scots Confession, the Heidelberg Catechism, the Second Helvetic Confession, the Westminster Confession of Faith, the Shorter and Larger Catechisms, the Theological Declaration of Barmen, the Confession of 1967, and A Brief Statement of Faith. The adoption of the *Book of Confessions* indicates both a broad appreciation of the Presbyterian heritage and an effort to express the faith in ways that meet contemporary need.

The presbyterian form of church organization was forged in the struggle to bring the Protestant Reformation to Geneva, Switzerland. The major insights of the Reformation had already been formulated by others, especially Martin Luther in Wittenberg, Germany, and Ulrich Zwingli in Zürich, Switzerland. The great principles of the Reformation, such as the authority of the Bible, the right of private judgment, justification by faith, the sanctity of common life, and the mutual ministry of all believers, were a part of the legacy John Calvin, spiritual father of Presbyterians, inherited from Luther, Zwingli, and others.

Calvin and Knox

John Calvin (1509–1564) was born in France and trained as a lawyer. When he came to Geneva, the Reformation had already begun there, but much work remained. Calvin was a gifted thinker, and writer of the first volume of *The Institutes of the Christian Religion*, a work that remains influential today. In Geneva, Calvin's already considerable reputation as a biblical scholar and theologian continued to grow, and the city became a theological center of the Reformation and a haven for persecuted Protestants from other countries.

One of the most distinguished refugees was a fiery Scot, John Knox (c. 1514–1572). As pupil and assistant to Calvin, Knox was preparing for his eventual return to his native Scotland and a confrontation with its Roman Catholic queen, Mary. At this time, England and Scotland were separate countries. While Mary professed allegiance to Rome and the Catholic faith, England had already rejected its allegiance to the pope. The ensuing struggle between the two countries was bitter, but Knox succeeded in reforming the Church of Scotland, and Mary's son, James (after whom the King James Version of the Bible is named), became Protestant king of the united countries of England and Scotland following the death of Elizabeth I of England.

Presbyterians in America

Presbyterianism was carried to America by a variety of immigrants—Dutch, English, Scottish, French, Swiss, and others. Congregations were established from New England to the Carolinas but particularly in the Middle Colonies.

Presbyterians played a prominent role in the Colonies' struggle for independence. John Witherspoon, a minister from Scotland who came to America to be president of the College of New Jersey (later known as Princeton University), was the only clergyperson but one of several Presbyterians to sign the Declaration of Independence.

The Civil War and several major theological controversies created a number of splits in the ranks of American Presbyterianism. Since 1865, however, a number of unions have taken place. Notable among these was the union in 1958 between the United Presbyterian Church of North America and the Presbyterian Church in the United States of America, which produced the largest Presbyterian group up to that time, the United Presbyterian Church in the United States of America. In 1983 this group unified with the former "Southern" Presbyterians to form the Presbyterian Church (U.S.A.).

Theological Foundations

Presbyterians are trinitarian Christians standing in the mainstream of Western Reformed tradition. This does not mean that there are no distinctions between Presbyterians and other Protestant religious bodies about basic doctrine, but such differences tend to be matters of accent and emphasis rather than of fundamental disagreement. An illustration of a particular emphasis may be seen in the Presbyterian teaching about the *sovereignty* of God. Sovereignty implies an exalted concept of God as the creator of the universe, the sustainer of all God has made, and the sole ruler of all things natural, human, and historical. While other churches, such as the United Methodist Church, stress the love of God and the warmhearted response of the believer, Presbyterians stress the righteousness of God and humanity's duty to obey.

Sin and Hope

Presbyterians regard the sinful nature of humanity with stark realism. An often-misunderstood phrase that belongs to this tradition is "total depravity." It does not mean that everything one thinks or wills or does is only evil. Rather, it means that sin corrupts all our faculties, so that none of them may be used to serve God perfectly. In God's eyes, even our best thoughts and deeds are never wholly pure.

Presbyterians have been accused of painting too bleak a picture of human nature. They are not pessimists, however, for they believe in a God who is not only righteous, but merciful as well. The gospel is the good news that God loves sinners. God does not condemn us for being what we are. God calls on us to confess our sin and trust God's grace. When we do so, the burden of guilt is lifted and we are empowered to do what by our own strength was previously impossible.

Presbyterians as a whole take their duties seriously and have tried to be righteous, moral, and diligent in the common walks of life. The purpose of such living is not to win God's favor, which has already been fully and freely given, but to express gratitude in lives that will please God.

Signs of the Church

Presbyterians hold that the true church is found where the gospel is truly preached and heard, where the sacraments are faithfully administered and received, and where due discipline enables the ministry of word and sacrament to occur.

This understanding means that the Presbyterian Church claims to be not the whole church, but only a part of the universal, visible church on earth. It seeks cooperation and fellowship with others who acknowledge Jesus Christ as Lord, as can be seen in its work in the Consultation on Church Union. It is committed to ecumenicity and interprets its global mission as one of partnership and sharing with others around the world in doing the work of Jesus Christ.

The *Book of Order* of the reunited Presbyterian Church emphasizes the inclusiveness and global nature of the church, encompassing people of all ages, ethnic groups, cultures, and conditions, wherever they may live. It calls for dialogue with and respect for those who are not Christian. It means standing with people who are oppressed—economically, politically, or religiously—and working for their freedom in justice.

Authority of Scripture

The use of the Bible among Presbyterians deserves special mention. All agree that the word of God is of highest significance. But all do not agree about what the word of God is or how it is to be interpreted. Some Presbyterians equate the word of God with the words of scripture and assert it is inerrant and infallible in a literal sense. Others advocate a broader and older view, recognizing Jesus Christ as the Word Incarnate, the one sufficient revelation of God. The Confession of 1967 declares, "The church has received the books of the Old and New Testaments as prophetic and apostolic testimony in which it hears the word of God and by which its faith and obedience are nourished and regulated."

Preaching and Worship

Historically, preaching has been emphasized in the Presbyterian Church. The pulpit and Bible are often central in its architecture. The proclamation of the word rightly includes teaching as well as preaching, reflecting the conviction that preparation of people to hear the word is as important as its declaration. Presbyterians have therefore been deeply involved in education of all kinds, including the founding and support of many colleges, universities, and seminaries in the United States and around the world.

Among Presbyterian constitutional documents is the Directory for Worship. This document sets out standards and practices for worship but does not require that these be followed. Sessions (congregational governing bodies) are given freedom regarding the form and order of worship in the congregation. As a result, wide variations occur in practice.

Sacraments: Baptism and the Lord's Supper

Two sacraments are affirmed by the Presbyterian Church—baptism and the Lord's supper. In the Presbyterian tradition, infants as well as adults are baptized. The congregation and the parents have a "special obligation" to lead the baptized person to "a personal response to the love of God," according to the Confession of 1967.

The Lord's supper was long a point of separation between the Presbyterian and Reformed churches and the Lutheran churches. The differences had to do chiefly with how Christ is understood to be present in the sacrament, whether his presence is "spiritual" or "real." Recent ecumenical discussions, however, have found these differences to be matters more of nuance than substance, and large segments of the two traditions now affirm each other's sacramental understanding.

Presbyterian Order

The Presbyterian principle for structure and government is to do all things "decently and in order." The very word *presbyterian* comes from the Greek word for "elder" and indicates a form of organization and governance that is based on rule by elected elders who represent the people. For many years the presbyterian system has recognized three offices—elders, deacons, and ministers of word and sacrament—who are ordained after election by the people. Ordination to these three offices is the same, although the requirements for them may differ, as do their functions in the church.

The presbyterian form, then, differs from the episcopal form, in which power is vested in a person (bishop), and the congregational form, where power is vested in the people. Presbyterian government is representative, not hierarchical or purely democratic. Authority in the presbyterian system resides in a system of interconnected "governing bodies." The congregation is ruled by the *session*, made up of elders elected by the people, with the pastor as moderator (presiding officer). This body is responsible for the life and work of the congregation—its worship, education, programs, and mission. It makes policy and decides issues.

The *presbytery* is a representative body composed of the ministers of word and sacrament who serve congregations within its bounds, and elder representatives from each congregation within the geographical area of the presbytery. Ministers of word and sacrament are members of the presbytery, not of congregations, and the consent of the presbytery is required for a change in the terms of their call to serve a particular congregation or for a change in location of their pastoral services.

The *synod* is a regional body, often encompassing several states. It has responsibility for the presbyteries within its bounds and helps to provide services that the individual presbyteries could not provide.

The most inclusive governing body is the *General Assembly*. This body is made up of an equal number of ministers and elders elected by the presbyteries. It meets at least every two years to debate denominational policy, to hear appeals, and to recommend programs, strategies, and resources for the denomination.

Seeking New Ways

The Presbyterian Church (U.S.A.) is open to change; eager to cooperate with the larger church; determined to venture and to disagree; committed to social justice and inclusiveness; and willing to risk, particularly when working in secular realms where the prophetic voice of the church may not be welcome. It seeks earnestly for new ways to fulfill Christ's mission for our time.

For Discussion

1. Which confessions do Lutherans and Presbyterians have in common? How important are such documents?

2. What similarities and differences do you see between Lutheran beliefs and those of the Presbyterian Church?

3. What do you see as the strengths of the presbyterian form of church organization?

For Further Study

- *Body and Soul: Reclaiming the Heidelberg Catechism* by M. Craig Barnes (Faith Alive, 2012)
- *On Being Presbyterian: Our Beliefs, Practices, and Stories* by Sean Michael Lucas (P&R, 2006)
- *Presbyterian Beliefs: A Brief Introduction* by Donald H. McKim (Geneva, 2003)
- *Presbyterian Questions, Presbyterian Answers: Exploring Christian Faith* by Donald H. McKim (Geneva, 2004)
- Presbyterian Church (U.S.A.) website: www.pcusa.org

Table of Comparison

	Presbyterians	Lutherans
Teachings	1. Regard the Bible as the "witness without parallel" to Jesus Christ, who is the one sufficient revelation of God.	1. Accept the Bible as the written witness to God's revelation of saving action through Jesus Christ.
	2. Accept the Nicene and Apostles' Creeds, the Scots Confession, the Heidelberg Catechism, the Second Helvetic Confession, the Westminster Confession and the Shorter Catechism, the Theological Declaration of Barmen, and the Confession of 1967.	2. Accept the creeds, the Augsburg Confession, and Luther's Small Catechism as basic summaries of the faith. Recognize the remainder of the *Book of Concord* as a valid interpretation of the faith of the church.
	3. Consider the sacraments visible signs of an invisible grace, confirming our faith in the proclaimed word.	3. Consider baptism and holy communion to be means of God's grace.
	4. Believe that in communion the body and blood of Christ are really present but are received spiritually.	4. Affirm the real presence of Christ in communion.
Type of Worship	Varies from liturgical to free, usually with sermon as the climax.	Liturgical with both word and sacrament together making a complete service.
Governance	Elders elected by the people share authority with ministers in four governing bodies.	Interdependent congregational, regional, national, and global expressions of the church are characterized by democratic decision making, strong ecumenical relationships, elected leadership, and an ordained ministry.
Statistics	Membership: 2,451,980 Congregations: 10,487	

CHAPTER 26

REFORMED CHURCH IN AMERICA

In the Reformed Church infants are baptized as heirs of the covenant of grace.

The Reformed Church in America is the oldest Protestant denomination in America with an uninterrupted ministry. The Dutch who settled New Amsterdam (now New York) organized the first Reformed church on this continent in 1628. Although the English took over the area in 1664 and English became the language of the land, the Reformed Church continued to use the Dutch language for nearly a century. (Note that in 1857 the Christian Reformed Church in North America split from the Reformed Church in America, in part over a theological dispute with roots in the Netherlands.)

Both historically and theologically, the Reformed Church in America stands in the Calvinist tradition of the Protestant Reformation, but it is not rigid as some churches in that tradition. It combines the doctrine of God's sovereignty with a warm evangelical doctrine of Christ and a strong witness to the power of the Holy Spirit.

The church is seen as the body of believers in Christ and their children. Two sacraments are practiced: baptism and the Lord's supper. Both are viewed as means of grace, signs and seals of God's covenant of grace with us. Infants are baptized as heirs of the covenant of grace. In this act, they are officially incorporated into the life of the Christian church. In regard to the Lord's supper, the Reformed Church speaks of Christ's presence in the elements of bread and wine in holy communion.

The Bible is confessed to be the word of God, inspired by God and written by human beings. The authority and infallibility of the Bible extend over all that God intends to say to us in it and all that the Bible intends to teach. Reformed churches also subscribe to the Heidelberg Catechism, a sixteenth-century document relating to Christian life and witness.

The way of worship is neither completely regulated nor completely free. Required liturgical forms are provided for the sacraments. In government, the presbyterian pattern is followed. Congregations are governed by a *consistory*, made up of the pastor and elected elders and deacons. A *classis* oversees the congregations in a local jurisdiction and in turn reports to one of seven regional *synods*. The General Synod is the churchwide policy maker.

The Reformed Church is generally an ecumenically minded denomination. It has been a member of both the National Council of Churches and the World Council of Churches since each was started and is included in the Formula of Agreement between various Reformed denominations and the Evangelical Lutheran Church in America.

For Discussion

1. Reflecting on the way language shaped the church in the United States, what similarities do you see between the Reformed Church and the Lutheran Church?

2. An emphasis on God's sovereignty is central for Reformed churches. Luther and his followers preferred to emphasize the cross of Christ. What strengths does each bring to the Christian life?

For Further Study

· *By Grace Alone: Stories of the Reformed Church in America* by Donald J. Bruggink and Kim N. Baker (Faith Alive, 2004)

· *The Good News We Almost Forgot: Rediscovering the Gospel in a 16th Century Catechism* by Kevin DeYoung (Faith Alive, 2012)

· *The Netherlands Reformed Church, 1571–2005,* Historical Series of the Reformed Church in America, by Karen Blei (Eerdmans, 2006)

· Reformed Church in America website: www.rca.org

Table of Comparison

	Reformed Church	Lutherans
Teachings	1. Accept the Bible as the word of God.	1. Accept the Bible as the written witness to God's revelation of saving action through Jesus Christ.
	2. Uphold trinitarian doctrine. Believe in the deity and humanity of Christ and accent both.	2. Same.
	3. Proclaim justification by God's grace, accepted by faith.	3. Proclaim justification by grace through faith.
	4. Celebrate two sacraments: baptism and holy communion. Consider them means of grace; speak of the presence of Christ in the Lord's supper.	4. Celebrate two sacraments: baptism and holy communion. Consider them means of grace; affirm the real presence of Christ in the Lord's supper.
Type of Worship	Worship is semi-liturgical; for the sacraments, forms are fixed; great freedom in other parts of the church's worship.	Liturgical, following classic traditions and services of the Western church. Preaching of the word and celebration of sacrament are main events of worship.
Governance	Presbyterian pattern used with representative church government. Church is ruled by elders, with clergy considered teaching elders.	Interdependent congregational, regional, national, and global expressions of the church are characterized by democratic decision making, strong ecumenical relationships, elected leadership, and an ordained ministry.
Statistics	Membership: 295,120 Congregations: 864	

CHAPTER 27

RELIGIOUS SOCIETY OF FRIENDS

Friends believe that God can speak to anyone directly. In their meetings for worship, anyone may stand up to speak or pray.

Quakers are often associated with a quaint, old-fashioned people who centuries ago came with William Penn to found the colony of Pennsylvania, but Quakers today are in tune with the current religious environment. Drawing on their tradition, they want to minimize distinctions between clergy and laity. They give equal recognition and responsibilities, including the ministry, to men and women. They have pioneered in addressing social injustices and human exploitation. They have readily found genuine Christian fellowship in small informal groups working and worshiping together. They have cherished a freedom to express their convictions without being boxed in by creeds and ritual.

They are, however, still a small group. Being a Quaker is not easy, because their convictions often differ from popular attitudes about militarism, gambling, and personal moral behavior. To be a Quaker calls for a higher degree of individual responsibility, initiative, and integrity than many church members are ready to exercise. Quakers in America today are divided into various groups as a result of theological controversies.

History of the Friends

Their name Friends comes from Jesus' words, "You are my friends if you do what I command you" (John 15:14). The term *Quaker* came about because their founder, George Fox, once scolded a judge for an unfair sentence by saying he should quake (tremble) before the Lord for handing out such a sentence as an example of justice.

Fox was a young man who did not like what he saw being done in the name of the church in his day. He lived in England in the seventeenth century, a time of great religious and political turmoil. To some people, the established church seemed to substitute rituals for inward religious experience and personal integrity, and they began seeking a religion of genuine personal experience in direct communion with God. Fox was among these seekers. He went to the clergy for help and was advised, for example, that he should have some blood drained, chew tobacco, and get married to find inner peace. After these disappointments, he sought help directly from God. It came to him in a profound religious experience in which he heard a voice within saying, "There is one, even Christ Jesus, who can speak to thy condition." He was elated to find the way to direct communion with God.

Fox was twenty-three years old when he began preaching with great joy about his discovery that Christ was available to be any person's teacher. This was a revolutionary discovery for his day, and he soon ran into strong opposition. Thousands of Friends were jailed and their property taken. They were persecuted (hundreds died in prison, and several were hanged) because they would not conform to their country's religious and political establishments.

Because of the persecution, great numbers of early Friends came to America to enjoy religious and political freedom. Not only was Pennsylvania a Quaker stronghold, but the colonies of Rhode Island, New Jersey, Maryland, and North Carolina also had large Quaker populations and were ruled by Quaker governors with Quaker majorities in their early representative bodies. By the time Fox died in 1691, there were nearly fifty thousand Friends in England, Europe, and colonial America. In the United States, largely through the work of John Woolman, all Quakers freed their slaves some seventy years before the Civil War.

Theology: Faith to Work

Friends hold many beliefs in common with other Christian denominations; however, they have not placed as much stress on theology as on putting their faith to work. Friends have sometimes described Christ living within the person of faith as the Light within. Friends believe that every person is born with an inner capacity to respond to God's Spirit without having a minister act as a go-between. Salvation is seen as a process of obedient living that begins with a conscious commitment to be a follower of Christ.

Although Friends are optimistic about a person's capacity to do good, they believe everyone has to accept God's redemptive, loving Spirit into his or her life before the tenacious power of sin and the haunting fear of death can be overcome. Once the inward Light of Christ is a part of a person's life, though, it will result in peace, integrity, equality, and community.

Although most Friends support the doctrine of the Trinity, they prefer focusing attention on God's action in the world rather than formulating a statement about God's nature. Some liberal Friends prefer a unitarian understanding of God to the trinitarian.

Church: People in Fellowship

The church is a people of God called into fellowship, worship, and service in order to make God's love known in this world. Friends have used the word *church* only to describe the fellowship of believers. The congregation is called a meeting, and their place of worship is a meetinghouse. They describe their weekly services as meetings for worship, when they come together to meet in the presence of Christ. They call themselves a Religious Society of Friends instead of a church because they believe only God can create the church.

Friends rely on the scriptures as inspired and as one of the primary channels of God's revealed truth, but not the exclusive revelation of truth. A small number of Friends hold to a literalistic interpretation of the Bible. Quakers believe in the continuing revelation of truth through the inspiration of the Holy Spirit.

Friends do not use creeds, holding that all believers should be free to describe their own convictions on the basis of their own religious experience rather than using someone else's words. Although this view allows considerable freedom, Friends are expected to use a set of carefully prepared questions for periodic self-examination to see if they are faithfully participating in the movement of Friends.

No Sacraments

Friends do not observe any of the traditional sacraments. They believe that all of life—not just special days, people, or rituals—is sacred. They believe the inward baptism of the Spirit is the heart of personal religious experience and that a ceremony using water is not essential. They believe in the communion of a worshiping congregation with the Spirit of the risen Christ and that it is not necessary to use the symbols of bread and wine to participate in this experience. Friends assert that Jesus did not explicitly teach any of these ceremonies.

Ministry and Worship

The Friends' view of ministry and worship differs from traditional Protestant views. They believe that all believers are called to be ministers by using their spiritual gifts. Believing that God can speak directly to anyone, in their meetings for worship they allow anyone to stand up to speak or pray as he or she may feel inspired by the Spirit of Christ.

The traditional meeting for worship proceeds without a planned order of service. The worshipers gather quietly in the meeting room and consciously turn their minds to prayer and meditation. Elders sit at the front, facing the congregation, and are responsible for maintaining the quiet dignity of the meeting. Should anyone take advantage of this freedom to participate by speaking in a way that is obviously not in the spirit of worship, an elder may gently interrupt and ask the speaker to sit down.

A majority of the Friends meetings in the United States now have pastors. The Friends pastor, who may be a man or a woman, carries out many of the same functions as a Protestant clergyperson, but there are some distinct differences. He or she leaves time in the meetings of worship for others to participate. Occasionally the pastor may not speak at all if he or she does not feel truly inspired. The primary role of the pastor is to detect the undeveloped spiritual gifts in others and to help each member more fully employ them. The pastor sees himself or herself as part of a team ministry in partnership with other gifted members.

The local meeting is the basic governing body in the Religious Society of Friends, subject to the authority of the regional Yearly Meeting. All the members may participate in the monthly business meeting presided over by a clerk. There is no voting; decisions are reached only when the whole body is persuaded that they are responding obediently to the leading of the Spirit.

Peacemakers

Friends have throughout their history worked at being peacemakers, both by binding up the wounds of war in relief services and by trying to remove the causes of war. They believe that to kill another human being under any circumstance is evil because every person is a child of God. They support the use of restraint and police force to protect the innocent and to provide opportunity for the aggressor to transform into a useful, responsible citizen. Friends' belief in the sacredness of all life has made them leaders in movements to eliminate racial discrimination and to secure the rights of all people.

The American Friends Service Committee is widely known for its peacemaking and social reform services. It is an independent agency under the direction of a Quaker board. In all of the Friends' involvement in the community and world, they try to faithfully express their religious life and experience and contribute toward God's kingdom among humankind.

For Discussion

1. Friends emphasize right living over right belief. What are the advantages and dangers of such an approach?

2. Martin Luther warned against those who looked for individual revelation rather than seeking God in the Bible or the church. Do you think such concerns are justified?

3. Compare the Quaker tradition of pacifism with the approach of your church.

For Further Study

· *Imagination and Spirit: A Contemporary Quaker Reader* by J. Brent Bill (Friends United, 2003)

· *An Introduction to Quakerism* by Pink Dandelion (Cambridge University Press, 2007)

· *A Quaker Book of Wisdom: Life Lessons in Simplicity, Service, and Common Sense* by Robert Lawrence Smith (William Morrow, 1999)

· Religious Society of Friends website: www.quaker.org

Table of Comparison

	Friends	Lutherans
Teachings	1. Accept the scriptures as inspired but not exclusive revelation of truth.	1. Accept the scriptures as the written witness to God's revelation of saving action through Jesus Christ.
	2. Believe in Christ as Lord and Savior.	2. Same.
	3. Teach responsible obedience to the leading of the Holy Spirit.	3. Same.
	4. Do not consider traditional sacraments as necessary to salvation.	4. Consider sacraments of baptism and holy communion to be channels of God's grace for the salvation of humankind.
	5. Believe that the sacredness of all human life does not allow anyone to exploit or destroy another.	5. Historically grant the need for law and force in governing all people on earth. Such an attitude admits the possible necessity of war.
Type of Worship	Informal with simplicity and dignity with a minimum of prearranged order. Worshipers may speak or pray as they feel inspired. Some meetings are presided over by a pastor who shares with others in the ministry.	Liturgical forms used for the sake of good order. People are involved in dialogue of liturgical worship led by a pastor, who is trained and called to the public office of the ministry on behalf of the people.
Governance	Local meeting (congregation) is autonomous. All members may participate in monthly business meetings presided over by a clerk. There is no voting. Relationship to large bodies is through representation and recommendation, not by centralized control.	Interdependent congregational, regional, national, and global expressions of the church are characterized by democratic decision making, strong ecumenical relationships, elected leadership, and an ordained ministry.
Statistics*	Membership: 97,019 Congregations: 1,186	

*Figures include the four largest Friends groups in the United States.

CHAPTER 28

ROMAN CATHOLIC CHURCH

The Roman Catholic Church recognizes the pope as the successor of Peter and chief teacher and shepherd of the church.

Many of the church bodies discussed in this book trace their roots back to the Roman Catholic Church. Those who have studied the history of the Reformation may be aware of the problems that led to those divisions, but the Roman Catholic Church today is a much different institution from that of the Reformation era.

The transition to modern Catholicism began in the nineteenth century. Already then, Catholic theologians were beginning to closely examine the biblical nature of the church as the body of Christ, his living presence in the world. Several forces, including biblical, theological, liturgical, and social movements, prepared the Roman Catholic Church and its members for change. All this preparation bore fruit in the mid-twentieth century in an important worldwide church council commonly called Vatican II.

The Second Vatican Council was a council of reform. This reform was not aimed so much at correcting obvious abuses, as existed at the time of Martin Luther; rather, the Council sought to renew the very idea of religious practice, belief, and worship. Since then, these concepts have been brought to reality.

Foundation of the Church

Catholics believe that the Roman church grew out of Jesus' formation of the apostles into a community. Through this community he would continue to teach and sanctify people until the end of time. From among the apostles, Jesus chose Peter (the name means "rock") to be the solid foundation for his church, the one who would take the Lord's own place when he would leave this world. This is one Catholic interpretation of Matthew 16:16-20. Catholics further believe that Jesus confirmed his choice of Peter after the resurrection when he told Peter, "Feed my lambs . . . tend my sheep" (John 21:15-18). After presiding over the church at Jerusalem and Antioch for some years, Peter went to Rome as the first "bishop" of the Christian community in that city. Catholic teaching claims that since then, the bishops of Rome have succeeded to the office of Peter as the chief teacher and shepherd of the church.

The growth of the church over the centuries has been both human and divine. It has grown numerically and in depth, penetrating humankind with the mind of Christ. At the same time, it has been subject to human weaknesses and has experienced corruption. Catholics believe, however, that despite all the defects of the members of the church and even popes, the promise of Jesus has been maintained. The powers of death have not prevailed against it, nor will they.

Mystery of God

In common with most Christian denominations, the Roman Catholic Church believes in the doctrine of the Trinity as taught by Jesus. The Trinity is a "mystery." That is, humans could not have known of it without divine revelation, and even with that revelation, it cannot be wholly understood. But simply stated, the doctrine of the Trinity means that one God exists in three "people." The three people share one divine nature and therefore are equally eternal and almighty.

The Father, as described in the Gospels, guides and watches over his children, forgives them when they stray, and cares for them in all their need. He is also the great king who watches over the earth. In Jesus, the Son of God, God becomes visible. The Son became human; that is, he became like us in all things except sin. Dying on the cross and rising from death, Jesus restored the possibility of living forever with God. The Holy Spirit is the personification of the mutual love between the Father and the Son and is the life principle of the body of Christ, the church. It is the Spirit who gives us a taste for God and God's word and who makes us capable of living in love. The Spirit is responsible for the urge among Christians to come together in unity.

Salvation from God

The Roman Catholic Church believes that Jesus is the only Savior of humankind. Salvation is the free gift of God that can in no way be merited by any human work. Humankind, which in some mysterious way was cut off from God and immersed in evil, is restored in Christ by his saving word and deed—his entire life, death, and resurrection.

Although everyone is considered a member of redeemed humanity, the Roman Catholic Church teaches that simple membership in the church does not automatically imply salvation. Each person is responsible for his or her own life and the manner in which he or she responds to Christ. As Jesus often warned, anyone can be lost, choosing eternal separation from God and from fellowship with God's people.

Even though some people may give the impression that they can work out their own salvation by following rules and laws, performing religious rites, and practicing self-denial, the Roman Catholic Church teaches that Christ alone saves. The person's only task is to accept that salvation with loving trust.

The Church: God's People

Despite how it may appear at times, the church is not at heart simply an organization. It is the mystery of the people of God. Its purpose is to bear witness to Christ and to be Christ to the nations.

Just as the humanity of Christ is the sacrament—the effective sign, the manifestation—of the Father, so the church is the sacrament of Christ. And the sacraments in turn are the manifestation of the church. As Christ acted on people by word and deed during his life on earth, so he now acts through the sacraments in the church that are the extension of his humanity.

The task of bishops and priests is to be Christ to their people—to proclaim his word and to bring the very life of God by means of the sacraments. Above all, they are to preside over the eucharist, holy communion, so the people may personally enter into Christ's redeeming work and make it their own.

Sacraments: Sacred Signs

The sacraments are sacred signs of spiritual strength, healing, and food whereby Jesus enters personally into the lives of Christians. By the power of Christ, sacraments accomplish what they signify. For instance, baptism is the sign of cleansing and dying with Christ in order to rise with him, and through Christ's power that dying and rising becomes real. The eucharist not only offers food and nourishment, but also provides spiritual food, the body and blood of Jesus, the bread of life.

The sacraments bring God's grace to bear at various points in life. Baptism corresponds to birth or adoption into a human family or becoming a naturalized citizen. Through baptism, we become members of the family of God. Confirmation functions as a bridge between baptism and the eucharist, as the maturing Christian moves deeper into the faith. Penance meets the needs of a person who falls into sin; Christ heals the sinner and restores him or her to healthy membership in the people of God. Eucharist corresponds to the need of every human being for food on the journey of life. And in any serious illness, in a person's most desperate need, Christ comes to him or her in the sacrament of the anointing of the sick to strengthen and comfort—and often to restore the sick person to health. Finally, in the sacraments of matrimony and orders, the recipient gives oneself in service. In matrimony, Christ enters into the lives of husbands and wives, joins them in love for one another and for him, and gives them courage and help necessary to be faithful to their difficult vocation. And in orders, Jesus chooses men, even as he chose the apostles, to do what he has done: "As the Father has sent me, so I send you" (John 20:21).

The Mass

The primary worship service of the Roman Catholic Church is called the Mass. It has two parts: the Liturgy of the Word and the Liturgy of the Eucharist. In the Liturgy of the Word, the assembly focuses on God's word through hearing and responding to readings from the Bible, prayers of petition and praise, and the homily. The Liturgy of the Word prepares the people for the second part of the Mass, the Liturgy of the Eucharist, which includes prayers of praise and thanksgiving, offering, petition, and remembrance. Its heart is the recital by the priest, speaking in the name of the assembly, of the Eucharistic Prayer, which includes an account of the last supper. Then those present who wish to do so receive Jesus as food for their souls and for their daily living in their families and communities.

Pope and Bishops

Since Vatican II, the idea of collegial, or shared, authority has increasingly come to the fore. This model is at work in many situations. The pope and bishops gather in "general councils," such as Vatican II. The Synod of Bishops elected by national governing groups around the world meets regularly with the pope as a kind of senate to discuss problems relating to beliefs and practices of Catholics. Diocesan (area) synods of priests help their bishops shepherd, serve, and teach the faithful. Parish councils of laity chosen by fellow parishioners help the pastor with the spiritual and temporal administration of the parish.

Catholics believe that among the bishops, the pope holds special duties and privileges. One of the chief functions of the pope is that of teacher. He is the head of the College of Bishops and therefore possesses in a special measure divine protection from teaching error. Catholics do not believe this infallibility means the pope is incapable of sinning or erring in matters other than doctrine. Infallibility is not a personal quality of the pope. It belongs to his office and is only for the benefit of the people of God.

Points of Difference

Perhaps more than any other doctrine, this concept of authority in the church, centering in the papacy, distinguishes Catholics from Protestants. It is often the least understood teaching.

Another point of difference has to do with the virgin Mary. Catholics believe that Mary was a virgin before, during, and after the birth of her Son Jesus, though the "before" is stressed more than the "during" and "after." The "brothers and sisters" of Jesus mentioned in the Gospels are thought to have been his relatives, not his blood brothers and sisters, for the word *brothers* in Aramaic can also be used for relatives.

Catholics further believe that Mary was "conceived immaculately" in the womb of her mother. The immaculate conception is not the same as the virgin birth, which refers to Christ's being conceived and born of Mary without human intercourse. The immaculate conception simply means that Mary was conceived in her mother's womb without original sin, or to state it positively, that from the first moment of existence, she was redeemed. Catholics believe finally that Mary's body was assumed into heaven by the power of God at the moment of her death. This is the doctrine of assumption.

The scriptural source of Catholic beliefs concerning Mary is to be found at least implicitly in Luke 1–2. Official teaching places her in the first rank of redeemed Christians, not a "fourth person" of the Trinity, but a human being. Yet she was a human being loved by her Son and raised to her dignity only because she was the perfect Christian, the one who best fulfilled Jesus' own idea of sanctity.

Pilgrimage in the World

The Roman Catholic Church encourages its members to enter into the life of the secular city and to exercise their rights of citizenship in their nation. It has lived with every kind of political situation from the time of the Roman Empire, through feudalism and monarchies, to modern democracies. As Vatican II reminded members, the church has the duty to build a better world based on truth and justice. Since that council, a number of influential social teachings have promoted matters such as the dignity of every human being, the importance of human rights, and solidarity with suffering people throughout the world. Christians on their pilgrimage toward the heavenly city should seek and savor the things that are above. At the same time, they are obligated to work with all people in constructing a more humane world.

For Discussion

1. Did you grow up with prejudice or misinformation about Catholic beliefs and practices? If so, talk about that experience.

2. The Roman Catholic Church is the "mother church" for most Western denominations. Do you see your own church as being more similar to or different from this one?

3. What are your own thoughts and beliefs regarding the authority of the pope, the status of Mary, and other points of difference? How important are those differences?

For Further Study

- *Catholicism: A Very Short Introduction* by Gerald O'Collins (Oxford University Press, 2008)
- *An Invitation to the Catholic Faith: Exploring the Basics* by Joseph Stoutzenberger (Twenty-Third Publications, 2013)
- *The Seeker's Catechism: The Basics of Catholicism* by Michael Pennock (Ave Maria, 2012)
- United States Conference of Catholic Bishops website: www.usccb.org

Table of Comparison

	Roman Catholics	Lutherans
Teachings	1. Believe in the triune God.	1. Same.
	2. Believe in the full divinity and full humanity of Christ.	2. Same.
	3. Accept the Bible as the source of truth interpreted in the light of tradition.	3. Accept the Bible as the source of truth expressed in the creeds and confessions of tradition.
	4. Celebrate seven sacraments: baptism, confirmation, penance, eucharist, marriage, orders, and anointing of the sick.	4. Celebrate two sacraments: baptism and the eucharist.
	5. Believe in the real presence of Jesus in the consecrated bread and wine—that bread and wine are changed into the body and blood of Christ.	5. Believe in the real presence of Jesus in the eucharist. Each communicant receives not only the bread and wine but also the body and blood of Christ.
Type of Worship	Mass celebrated in the language of the people. Two main sections: word and sacrament. Order of Mass is the Western church pattern.	Liturgy is basically the same as Roman Catholic, but congregations have freedom to enrich the pattern.
Governance	College of Bishops shares authority with the pope as head of the college.	Interdependent congregational, regional, national, and global expressions of the church are characterized by democratic decision making, strong ecumenical relationships, elected leadership, and an ordained ministry.
Statistics	Membership: 58,963,835 Congregations: 20,589	

CHAPTER 29

SALVATION ARMY

William and Catherine Booth believed that a hungry person must be fed before he or she will hunger for the word of God.

The Salvation Army has, through the years of its existence, faced changing and expanding problems in society while still keeping its evangelical intent in the forefront. Preserving its individuality in worship and methods, it has become increasingly involved in programs and services consistent with its purpose of ministering to the spiritual and physical needs of humanity.

The Salvation Army believes in the fellowship and unity of all believers; however, because of its particular organization, worship, and doctrine, the Army continues to hold to its identity as a church.

Booth and the War against Evil

The misery of people living in poverty in London's East End moved William and Catherine Booth to dedicate their lives to the poverty-stricken and unchurched people of that area. Earlier, in 1861, as an ordained Methodist minister, William Booth had left the pulpit to become an evangelistic preacher. However, his confrontation with poverty in 1865 changed the course of his life.

The Booths initially intended to supplement the work of regular churches. All too often, however, converts were not accepted in these churches. The Booths soon found that rather than sending converts out of the neighborhood, they needed them to help handle the great crowds that attended their meetings. The work started under the name of the Christian Mission, but the name was changed in 1878 to the Salvation Army.

After the movement's name was changed, a new theme dominated the organization's work. A declaration of faith, called the "Articles of War," was developed. Booth was called a general, and a quasi-military pattern of authority was formulated. Mission stations became corps, members became soldiers, evangelists became officers, and converts were called prisoners. Booth sought to develop an army of crusaders to save people in the "war" against evil.

Once committed to a "military" policy of expansion, Booth began to send officers and soldiers throughout the world. The Army quickly spread. Today the Salvation Army works in 126 countries with about twenty-six thousand officers who preach the gospel in some 175 languages at 15,409 evangelical centers. The Army also operates more than ten thousand social welfare institutions, hospitals, schools, and other centers.

Although the Army functions as both a church and a social agency, its primary purpose is the salvation of humankind "by the power of the Holy Spirit combined with the influence of human ingenuity and love." Converts who want to become soldiers (members) of the Salvation Army must sign the "Articles of War." These articles are the conditions of membership. Enrollment as a member of the Army then occurs in a public ceremony. Volunteer service for Army work is expected of the new soldiers. The function of the Salvation Army officers is similar to that of ministers in other denominations. These officers are ordained and commissioned for full-time service.

Eleven Doctrines

The Salvation Army's constitution, originating in Christian Mission days, developed through a series of documents culminating in The Salvation Army Act 1980. This document gives the Salvation Army the legal status and power it needs to continue its work for the honor and glory of God. Included in the Act are the eleven cardinal doctrines of the Salvation Army, including the Army's affirmation of the Bible as the only rule of Christian faith and practice (God as creator and Father of all). Other affirmations include the doctrine of the Trinity, Christ's humanity and divinity, sin as the great destroyer of a person's soul and society, salvation as God's answer to the sins of humankind, hope available through Christ, the maturing experience of a life consecrated for the holy purposes of God's kingdom, and an eternal destiny of victory over sin and death. The Methodist beliefs of the founder are reflected in the group, including an emphasis on complete sanctification or holiness.

The Booths believed that the sacraments are not essential to the salvation of the soul; therefore, the Army does not observe them. This feature of the Army distinguishes this group from most other Christian communities.

Extensive Social Work

A significant program of social welfare is carried on by the Salvation Army and financed through the voluntary offerings of its members and contributions from the general public. The importance of the social welfare program to the soldiers of the Army is clearly stated in the following excerpt from the Salvation Army mission statement:

> The Salvation Army, an international movement, is an evangelical part of the universal Christian church. Its message is based on the Bible. Its ministry is motivated by the love of God. Its mission is to preach the gospel of Jesus Christ and to meet human needs in His name without discrimination.

The Booths' belief that a hungry person must be fed before he or she will hunger for the word of God undergirds the practice of the Army even today.

For Discussion

1. How do you react to the Salvation Army's quasi-military organization and style?

2. The Salvation Army is best known for its social work. How important do you think such activity is for church bodies?

3. What do you think about the Salvation Army's nonuse of baptism and communion?

For Further Study

· *Christianity in Action: The International History of the Salvation Army* by Henry Gariepy (Eerdmans, 2009)

· *Red-Hot and Righteous: The Urban Religion of the Salvation Army* by Diane Winston (Harvard University Press, 2000)

· Salvation Army website: www.salvationarmyusa.org

Table of Comparison

	Salvation Army	Lutherans
Teachings	1. Accept the Bible as the word of God.	1. Accept the Bible as the written witness to God's revelation of saving action through Jesus Christ.
	2. Teach justification by faith.	2. Teach justification by grace through faith.
	3. Believe in the full divinity and humanity of Christ.	3. Same.
	4. Do not observe sacraments.	4. Celebrate two sacraments as means of God's grace: baptism and holy communion.
Type of Worship	Nonliturgical with much freedom for member participation. Simple, direct appeal to personal decision to follow Christ.	Liturgical, following the classical form of the Western church. Member participation in dialogue between the pastor and people in worship.
Governance	Quasi-military, authoritarian in structure but democratic in principle.	Interdependent congregational, regional, national, and global expressions of the church are characterized by democratic decision making, strong ecumenical relationships, elected leadership, and an ordained ministry.
Statistics	Membership: 379,031 Congregations: 1,234	

CHAPTER 30

SEVENTH-DAY ADVENTIST CHURCH

Tithing, giving one-tenth of a person's income, is an important practice of the Seventh-day Adventist Church.

The first part of the name Seventh-day Adventist reflects the belief that Christians are still bound to keep the seventh day of the week as the sabbath; the second part refers to the advent, or coming, of Christ. Seventh-day Adventists believe that all sincere Christians constitute the invisible church, but they also believe that the Seventh-day Adventist Church has been given a special message to proclaim to the world in this generation. This message is the everlasting gospel of Jesus Christ and the announcement of Christ's return.

The message calls for immediate preparation for what is believed to be Christ's imminent, personal, visible return to earth in glory and power to establish his universal and eternal reign. Seventh-day Adventists see in the modern world continual reminders of Christ's challenge to discern "the signs of the times" (Matthew 16:2-3; see also 2 Timothy 3:1-5). Expanded technology, burgeoning population, and social upheavals all contribute to this awareness for the Seventh-day Adventist.

The Church's Beginnings

This church is a conservative Christian body, extending throughout the world. It considers itself evangelical in doctrine and professes no creed except the Bible. It dates back to a time of widespread interest during the eighteenth and nineteenth centuries in the second advent of Christ. Followers of evangelist William Miller, called Millerites, expected Christ's return between March 21, 1843, and March 21, 1844. When the dates proved incorrect, a later date was set, but again the day of the Lord failed to appear as expected.

A series of conferences under the leadership of James and Ellen White and Joseph Bates led to the fusion of isolated groups of sabbath-keeping Adventists in New York and New England. Between 1848 and 1850, most differences were resolved, and the main teachings and beliefs were formulated and then further developed during the 1850s.

Most of this work was carried out in periodical articles and pamphlets on various Bible subjects, often written in response to the claims of their opponents. At a general meeting in 1860 at Battle Creek, Michigan, the denominational name of Seventh-day Adventists was adopted. Then in 1863 a general conference convened and framed the church constitution.

Central Doctrines

The beliefs of the Seventh-day Adventists depend heavily on the apocalyptic books of Daniel and Revelation. Distinctive emphases include a two-phase ministry of Jesus Christ as humanity's high priest in the heavenly sanctuary, an "investigative judgment" in the heavenly sanctuary prior to the second advent, esteem for the witness of Ellen G. White as a special messenger, and the messages of the three angels in Revelation 14.

Seventh-day Adventists believe that the holy scriptures of the Old and New Testaments were given by God's inspiration and contain a revelation of God's will to humanity. They believe the Bible's teaching about the Trinity, and they believe that the universe and the world were created and are sustained by God through Christ. God created the world in six days and not through a long evolutionary process. Because of sin humanity lost its original state of perfection, but by faith in Jesus Christ human beings may be saved—renewed and restored by the transforming power of the Holy Spirit to enjoy eternal life—all through the grace of God. Salvation is a gift through faith in the righteousness of Christ. Keeping the Ten Commandments is a response to the love of Christ and his sacrifice on the cross.

Seventh-day Adventist beliefs are in harmony with historic Christianity as expressed in the Apostles' Creed, but the church does not hold to any creed. Before candidates are received into church membership, however, they affirm a series of beliefs and practices.

Baptism by immersion, holy communion and foot washing, tithing (a tithe is one-tenth of a person's income), and nonliturgical services are characteristic. Members tend to take religion personally and seriously in regard to time, possessions, and health. They eat and dress simply and avoid things found to be harmful to mental and physical health, such as tobacco, alcoholic beverages, drugs, certain meats, and excesses of any kind.

The State and God

Church members are active in community health, welfare, and disaster programs. Believing that people have a twofold duty to God and state, the Seventh-day Adventist Church affirms that God has delegated to civil government authority and jurisdiction in temporal, earthly matters; however, only God has authority and jurisdiction over a person's conscience. In the best interests of both church and state, civil government must observe strict neutrality in religious matters, neither promoting religion nor restricting individuals or the church in the legitimate exercise of their rights to religious freedom.

For Discussion

1. This denomination arose out of a belief that Christ would return very soon. How do you respond to people who hold such beliefs?

2. Though many Christians enjoy Saturday worship, how would you answer the claim that because of the sabbath commandment, that is the day on which all Christians should worship?

For Further Study

- *A Brief History of Seventh-day Adventists*, 2nd ed., by George R. Knight (Review and Herald, 2013)

- *A Search for Identity: The Development of Seventh-day Adventists Beliefs*, Adventist Heritage Series, by George R. Knight (Review and Herald, 2000)

- Seventh-day Adventist website: www.adventist.org

Table of Comparison

	Seventh-day Adventists	Lutherans
Teachings	1. Accept the Bible as the word of God and believe in continuing the spirit of prophecy.	1. Accept the Bible as the written witness to God's revelation of saving action through Jesus Christ. All subsequent revelation must be interpreted in light of God's central revelation in Jesus Christ.
	2. Accept the Trinity and the atonement of Christ.	2. Same.
	3. Practice baptism, holy communion, and foot washing.	3. Celebrate sacraments of baptism and holy communion.
	4. Regard observance of seventh-day sabbath as binding for all time.	4. Consider seventh-day sabbath as binding only for Old Testament times; Christ's resurrection is celebrated each Sunday.
	5. Consider tithing and dietary rules binding on Christians.	5. Stress the freedom of the Christian under the gospel.
Type of Worship	Nonliturgical.	Liturgical, following the classical form of the Western church.
Governance	Local churches have considerable power, but a type of representative government is used for the business of the church.	Interdependent congregational, regional, national, and global expressions of the church are characterized by democratic decision making, strong ecumenical relationships, elected leadership, and an ordained ministry.
Statistics	Membership: 1,194,996 Congregations: 5,665	

CHAPTER 31

UNITARIAN UNIVERSALIST ASSOCIATION

The lighting of a candle placed in a silver chalice is a central act of the worship service in many Unitarian Universalist congregations.

The history of Unitarian Universalism is that of a religious people challenging the authority of the church, its creeds, and its traditions. While these sources of authority were being challenged, the individual's ability to understand what is interpreted as the word of God, true, right, and good was affirmed. Reason was also defended as the basic criterion for judging religious truth and understanding scripture.

The movement called Unitarian Universalism began as a series of disconnected efforts to complete the Reformation. Of particular interest were the Trinity and the divinity of Christ. In 1531 Michael Servetus, a Spanish radical, challenged the traditional doctrine of the Trinity, arguing that there is no distinction of beings in God but only manifold aspects of deity. Francis David in Transylvania (present-day Romania) declared in 1569 that "the equality of Christ with God is only of a kind which God gave Christ, God remaining in his divine sovereignty above everyone else." The "unity" of God is preserved, leading to the name Unitarian.

During this period in the history of Christianity, differing points of view were not readily accepted in either the Roman Catholic or Protestant churches. In some areas, an individual challenging the accepted view of the church risked being labeled a heretic and exiled. The church and the state were not separate, so decisions made by church officials could affect the political rights of a citizen. An important and radical step toward religious freedom was taken when Francis David convinced King Sigismund of Transylvania to enact the first edict of religious tolerance in 1568. Michael Servetus did not have this freedom and was burned at the stake for his beliefs in Geneva, Switzerland. He is considered the first Unitarian martyr.

Reason and Belief

Unitarianism later emerged in England, again using reason in the interpretation of scripture, the purification of Christian doctrine, and the defense of religious liberty. John Locke, Isaac Newton, and Joseph Priestley (the leading spokesperson for Unitarianism as well as a noted scientist) were influential promoters of "the reasonableness of Christianity."

American Unitarianism, while influenced by European ideas, arose in New England as an indigenous movement of freedom of conscience and congregational independence. These Unitarians rejected doctrines such as predestination, total depravity, the Trinity, and eternal torment, while affirming a belief in the moral capacity of humans, the unity of God, the importance of reason, democracy in religion, and universal salvation. Its adherents opposed slavery as an insult not only to humans, but to the God in whose image they were created. Ralph Waldo Emerson, the famous American literary figure, began his career as a Unitarian minister, applying his ideas of transcendentalism to religion. His ideas were influential in Unitarianism as he stressed adding intuition to human reason as a way of discovering religious truth.

Universalist Roots

Universalism developed in eighteenth-century England. The conviction, rooted in 1 Corinthians 15:22 and other scripture texts, that God elects all humans to salvation was held in various forms by Origen of Alexandria, Gregory of Nyssa, and other church fathers. Proponents of universal salvation, abbreviated "Universalism," argued against the Calvinist belief that some are predestined to heaven and others are predestined to hell. John Murray is often credited with bringing Universalism from England to America at the end of the eighteenth century, although groups with universalist beliefs were present in America prior to his arrival. Universalism attracted thousands of converts on the American frontier during the nineteenth century.

The Unitarian and Universalist beliefs in a benevolent God and universal salvation gave these two groups a common ground during the nineteenth century. For several decades in the twentieth century, these two denominations worked toward a merger. This finally took place in 1961, resulting in the Unitarian Universalist Association.

Contemporary Attitudes and Practices

In accordance with the principle of individual freedom of belief, Unitarian Universalists hold widely varying convictions about themselves, their church, and the world. Within the circle, one can find Unitarian Universalist Christians, Buddhists, and pagans (embracing earth-centered spirituality), among others. Some of the most characteristic beliefs are summarized here.

Most Unitarian Universalists affirm God to be the evolutionary process by means of which the universe and humans came into being and tend toward perfection. For some, God is a reality to whom prayer is directed. For others, the word *God* is an abstract symbol for the unity of existence.

Unitarian Universalists regard Jesus as a human being. Some hold Jesus to be one figure in the line of world prophets extending from Moses and Buddha to Gandhi and Martin Luther King Jr. Christian-oriented Unitarian Universalists, a minority within the denomination, regard Jesus as the Christ who came to bring a new era to the world, an era whose vehicle is the church and whose consummation is reconciling love.

The church, for Unitarian Universalists, is an association of people who choose to unite for worship, personal growth, and social outreach. Being congregational in organization, each local group has full authority to determine its teachings and call a minister.

Unitarian Universalist worship expresses the particular faith of each congregation and its minister. There is no prayer book, no liturgical year, no mandatory sacrament. The sermon occupies a large place in worship. Unitarian Universalists are flexible in their worship. Some pray to God, others ponder the events of the day, others unite in what one minister calls the "sacrament of silence." Many congregations and ministers use dialogue or discussion sermons, sacred dance, jazz music, and the graphic arts.

Active in Society

Unitarian Universalists have always been at the forefront of humanitarian initiatives—historically in abolishing slavery, establishing universal education, ensuring voting rights for all adults, and improving conditions for people who are blind, those with mental illness, and those living in poverty. Today they work for the cause of peace, human rights, the right to choose abortion, separation of church and state, and gay rights.

Support of women's rights has long been a hallmark of the denomination. In fact, the Universalists were the first denomination to ordain a woman (Olympia Brown in 1863). The number of female ministers in the combined denomination dramatically increased in the late twentieth century, reaching 50 percent in 1999. This reflects consistent denominational support for the role of women in religion.

Although excluded on doctrinal grounds from most councils of churches, Unitarian Universalists maintain active and cordial relationships with other denominations. The National Council of Churches is represented by official observers at the annual General Assemblies of the Unitarian Universalist Association. Ministers are active in interfaith activities at many levels of church life, including ecumenical worship, study groups, and efforts for peace and social justice.

For Discussion

1. What in addition to reason do you think people rely on to determine belief?

2. How would you respond to the Universalist claim that God saves all people?

3. In what ways do you think your denomination should follow the example of the Unitarian Universalist Association? It what ways do you think it should not?

For Further Study

· *100 Questions That Non-Members Ask about Unitarian Universalism* by John Sias (Transition, 1994)

· *An Introduction to Unitarian and Universalist Traditions* by Andrea Greenwood and Mark W. Harris (Cambridge University Press, 2011)

· *Unitarian Universalism: A Narrative History* by David E. Bumbaugh (Meadville Lombard, 2001)

· *The Unitarian Universalist Pocket Guide*, 5th ed., ed. Peter Morales (Skinner House, 2012)

· Unitarian Universalist Association website: www.uua.org

Table of Comparison

	Unitarian Universalists	Lutherans
Teachings	1. Believe the Bible is a book written by humans that must be understood in its historical context.	1. Believe the Bible is the written witness to God's revelation of saving action through Jesus Christ.
	2. Reject creeds as a violation of reason, conscience, and experience.	2. Accept creeds as summaries of Christian truth.
	3. Affirm the unity of God.	3. Affirm the unity of the triune God.
	4. View Jesus as a great teacher and example, not a person of the Trinity.	4. Believe Jesus is both divine and human in nature, the second person of the Trinity, our Savior.
	5. Teach salvation by character: "You will know them by their fruits" (Matthew 7:16).	5. Teach salvation by grace through faith, a gift of God: "The one who is righteous will live by faith" (Romans 1:17b).
Type of Worship	Worship is more a celebration of the present than a memorial to the past. Historical and experimental forms are intermixed.	Worship is a celebration of God's grace and a confession of faith. Liturgical forms are used to glorify and thank God.
Governance	Freedom of individual conscience is secured in the independence of local congregations. Continental body is a democratic association of local churches and fellowships.	Interdependent congregational, regional, national, and global expressions of the church are characterized by democratic decision making, strong ecumenical relationships, elected leadership, and an ordained ministry.
Statistics	Membership: 211,606 Congregations: 1,022	

CHAPTER 32

UNITED CHURCH OF CHRIST

Sponsoring homes for children is one way the United Church of Christ works for justice and love in society.

Formed in 1957, the United Church of Christ (UCC) blends four distinct heritages within the Christian tradition. As a united and uniting church, it takes seriously the prayer of Jesus Christ "that they may all be one" (John 17:21). It affirms God's intention to reconcile the whole world to God and believes church unity contributes to this larger purpose. This search for unity has led to a variety of ecumenical relationships. It further recognizes that the primary force for change in the world and in the church is the activity of God, as God continually creates, judges, and redeems the world. Thus, it searches for and responds to signs of God's activity for justice and reconciliation in secular events as well as within the church.

As it focuses on God's work in our time, the United Church of Christ recognizes the importance of remembering how God has worked and the church has attempted to be faithful through the centuries. It affirms its own traditions, as well as its solidarity with all Christians from the earliest times. It also recognizes the need for continual change in the church if it is to remain faithful to the good news of God in Christ. It attempts to take its heritage seriously as well as to discern the shape of the future in order to live more faithfully in the present.

Four Streams of History

Two of the four major streams composing the United Church of Christ trace their roots to Reformation times in Europe. A third stream originated in England during the early seventeenth century, while the fourth stream is of purely American origin, dating from about the beginning of the nineteenth century.

One European stream was the Reformed churches in Switzerland, Germany, France (the Huguenots), and Hungary. Members from the German-speaking Reformed churches arrived in America in the early 1700s. These were followed during the next two hundred years by immigrants from the other countries. These Reformed groups brought with them the Heidelberg Catechism, written by Zacharias Ursinus and Caspar Olevianus under the inspiration of Lutheran reformer Philip Melanchthon.

The second continental stream resulted from the Prussian Union of 1817 between the Lutheran and Reformed churches. Beginning in the 1830s, many members of these Evangelical churches, as they were called, immigrated to the United States. One of their earliest acts after organizing in the 1840s was preparing the Evangelical Catechism, a synthesis of the Heidelberg Catechism and Luther's Small Catechism.

While the Reformed and Evangelical roots go back to the Reformation on the continent, the earliest forebears of the United Church of Christ to settle in this country were refugees and colonists from England. This third stream came from two chief groups: the Independents (later called the Pilgrims), who founded Plymouth Plantation in 1620, and the Puritans, who formed the Massachusetts Bay Colony in 1630. The Congregational churches grew out of the fusion of these two groups.

A fourth stream in the United Church of Christ developed during the late 1700s and early 1800s. Three groups of churches emerged as a result of splits from the Methodists in North Carolina, the Presbyterians in Kentucky, and the Baptists in New England. These groups were seeking to be faithful to what they held to be the essentials of New Testament Christianity. Within twenty years these groups had entered into fellowship, calling themselves the Christian Churches. Committed to unity in Christ, they affirmed the Bible as the sole source of tradition, dispensed with formal organizational structures, rejected doctrinal formulations, including that of the Trinity, and sought to live out the teachings of Jesus, guided by his divine Spirit. They required believer's baptism for entrance into the church, though people baptized in infancy were not excluded from the fellowship.

The Process of Union

For many years these four streams flourished separately on the American scene. In 1931 the Congregational churches and the Christian Churches formed the Congregational-Christian Churches. Shortly thereafter, in 1934, the Evangelical Synod of North America and the Reformed Church in the United States united to form the Evangelical and Reformed Church.

Early in the 1940s the two newly formed denominations began informal conversations about the possibility of eventual union. Despite major differences, these groups shared fundamental perceptions of what Christian faith and life were all about. Both recognized the sovereignty of God over the church and over human traditions and emphasized human freedom. Additionally, both groups were themselves the product of unions and had experience with the strengths and weaknesses of that process.

Theological Stance

With such a diverse background, there is no one "theology" of the United Church of Christ; however, it does have a distinctive theological stance. It recognizes that theological formulations are human attempts to state the significance of the gospel in terms that point beyond themselves to the working of God in history. It also recognizes that the theology one lives is more fundamental than the theology one professes.

In a broad sense, the United Church of Christ is trinitarian. The great majority of its members would affirm the sovereign love of God, the lordship of Christ, and the working of the Holy Spirit as descriptions of the one God, though the meaning and importance of each of these statements would vary greatly from person to person.

Human beings are created in God's image to live in fellowship with God and each other and to exercise stewardship over the rest of creation. Human sinfulness arises from lack of trust in God, which separates people from God and from their neighbor. This separation is overcome only through God's initiative toward humanity, shown in Jesus Christ.

Humankind's proper response to God involves one's whole life. It is not merely agreement with doctrine, nor passive acceptance of God's grace; rather, it is passionate commitment to justice and love among all people. Human beings do not earn their salvation by this involvement; this work is a liturgy of praise and thanksgiving for God's love.

The Church

The church is seen not so much as a company of the "saved," but as people who are servants of God in the service of humanity. As a community of faith, the church draws together in remembrance and hope to celebrate through its worship what God has done, is doing, and promises to do; to confess its lack of faith and its inadequate response to God's love; to ask for continued guidance, healing, and inspiration; and to serve humankind, thus witnessing to the redeeming love of God, who is the source of all meaning and power. Within the community, members share their experiences, nurture one another in Christian faith and life, and organize for common action in the world.

Within this doctrinal framework, the United Church of Christ gives concrete, institutional expression to the church. Organizationally, it recognizes itself as a distinct fellowship—a church—within the body of Christ. In this sense it is more than just a collection of congregations. It has its own integrity, symbolized by a constitution describing the free and voluntary relationships among the various groupings. Normally membership requirements consist of baptism—either infant or adult—and a public ceremony of intention to participate in the life of the church. Other requirements for membership vary from congregation to congregation.

There are four structural expressions of the church: the *congregation*, which is understood to be the primary form of the church; regional groups of congregations called *associations*, which are responsible for the standing of ministers and churches; *conferences*, which are statewide or larger groupings of congregations and associations responsible for the wider mission of the church; and the *General Synod* and related national bodies, which oversee global and national mission. Each of these settings of the church is autonomous in the matters for which it is responsible, but each lives in covenant relationship with all the other expressions of the church through elected representation, flow of information and opinions, program activities, and financial support.

Each congregation elects its own governing body, which may be called a church council, consistory, or board, depending on the historic tradition of the congregation. In many instances, boards of deacons, trustees, or elders are responsible for the spiritual life and fiscal affairs of the congregation. Ministers or pastors are called by vote of the entire congregation on the recommendation of pastoral search committees, with the assistance of the association or conference minister.

Priority Issues

Officially, the United Church of Christ is committed to active involvement in the social, cultural, and political issues of our time. In practice, however, the forms and the depth of this commitment vary greatly among the congregations.

Along with other denominations, the United Church of Christ gives special attention to racism, poverty, the environment, sexism, homosexuality, peace and justice, and the need to become a multicultural church. In 1985 the church's General Synod declared itself to be "open and affirming" and called on all settings of the church to welcome lesbian, gay, bisexual, and transgender people as full members of the church. Although congregations are free to determine their own mission in light of God's call, many congregations have declared themselves open and affirming regarding homosexuality, and gay and lesbian ordained ministers serve in the United Church of Christ.

Additional efforts range from establishing and supporting traditional social service agencies, such as hospitals, group homes, and care facilities for the elderly, to participating in movements for neighborhood renewal, political action on justice issues in every kind of governmental jurisdiction, and advocacy for people who are poor or oppressed, and those victimized because of gender, race, sexual orientation, handicapping conditions, or other circumstances.

National boards and agencies of the church disseminate studies and strategies concerning these issues to congregations so they can become agents of social change in their own communities, as well as help shape regional and national policy. Because each church is free to determine its own program and stance, however, not all UCC congregations agree with national church agencies on these matters and may choose to ignore or act against counsel from the wider church. Still, the guiding principle is that the body of Christ is called to witness to God's love and justice and to serve humankind. Only continuing repentance and the restoration of God's forgiving and gracious love can transform the church into an expression of God's purposes in the world.

For Discussion

1. How does the United Church of Christ's understanding of the importance of social ministry compare with that of your own denomination?

2. Do you think this denomination's history of unifying church bodies is a strength or a weakness? Why?

3. "Humankind's proper response to God . . . is passionate commitment to justice and love among all people." Do you agree or disagree with that statement? Why?

For Further Study

· *Theology and Identity: Traditions, Movements, and Polity in the United Church of Christ*, rev. ed., ed. Daniel L. Johnson and Charles Hambrick-Stowe (Pilgrim, 2007)

· *The Unofficial Handbook of the United Church of Christ* by Quinn G. Caldwell and Curtis J. Preston (Pilgrim, 2011)

· United Church of Christ website: www.ucc.org

Table of Comparison

	United Church of Christ	Lutherans
Teachings	1. Have no prescribed creeds. Statement of faith has been adopted, but is not binding. Teaching may vary from one congregation to another.	1. Use creeds, catechism, and confessions as summaries of the Bible's teachings. Congregations teach in accordance with Lutheran confessions.
	2. Most accept the Trinity, but interpretations vary.	2. Accept the doctrine of the Trinity.
	3. Most accept sacraments as signs of God's blessing.	3. Accept sacraments as channels of God's grace.
	4. Believe Christ's presence is celebrated in communion.	4. Believe in the real presence of Christ in the celebration of communion.
	5. Most rely on Christ's redemption for salvation.	5. Teach that people are saved by God's love as revealed in Christ.
Type of Worship	No set form of worship. Ranges from nonliturgical to liturgical.	Liturgical, following the classical form of the Western church.

Governance	Four structures: congregations, associations, conferences, and General Synod. Each is autonomous in its own sphere but in covenant relationship with other expressions.	Interdependent congregational, regional, national, and global expressions of the church are characterized by democratic decision making, strong ecumenical relationships, elected leadership, and an ordained ministry.
Statistics	Membership: 1,284,296 Congregations: 5,225	